D0773256

CM
12/93

THE COMPLEAT
CRUCIVERBALIST

THE COMPLEAT CRUCIVERBALIST

or

How to Solve and Compose Crossword Puzzles for Fun and Profit

Stan Kurzban
and
Mel Rosen

VNR VAN NOSTRAND REINHOLD COMPANY

NEW YORK   CINCINNATI   ATLANTA   DALLAS   SAN FRANCISCO
LONDON   TORONTO   MELBOURNE

Van Nostrand Reinhold Company Regional Offices:
New York Cincinnati Atlanta Dallas San Francisco

Van Nostrand Reinhold Company International Offices:
London Toronto Melbourne

Library of Congress Catalog Card Number: 80-12526
ISBN: 0-442-25738-4

Manufactured in the United States of America

Published by Van Nostrand Reinhold Company
135 West 50th Street, New York, N.Y. 10020

Published simultaneously in Canada by Van Nostrand Reinhold Ltd.

15 14 13 12 11 10 9 8 7 6 5 4 3 2 1

Library of Congress Cataloging in Publication Data
Kurzban, Stanley A.
  The compleat cruciverbalist.

  1. Crossword puzzles.   I.   Rosen, Mel, joint author.
II.   Title.
GV1507.C7K87   793.73′2   80-12526
ISBN 0-442-25738-4

To our fathers,
Alexander M. Kurzban and Robert L. Rosen,
who introduced us to word puzzles.

Foreword

The Messrs. Rosen and Kurzban obviously have been bitten by the puzzle bug and now they are trying to pass on their infection to as many others as they can. Since it is a relatively harmless plague, I hope it becomes epidemic. In my case it is too late because I have had the infection for many years and have developed into a terminal case.

One of the chief aims of the authors of this book is to make tigers out of pussycats in the matter of attacking crossword puzzles and allied brain teasers. A few hints here and there can do a lot toward building skill and confidence, and with it pleasure and self-gratification.

The word "pleasure" should have been underlined. The whole puzzle field is frothy and fleeting, and should never be taken too seriously. Is it a waste of time? Yes. But so is the whole spectrum of leisure activities. So crosswords need not be singled out.

Let's hope this book helps you waste that time painlessly.

Will Weng, former Puzzle Editor
for the *New York Times*

Preface

Crossword puzzles and related diversions provide countless hours of entertainment for people all over the world at relatively little cost. Many books contain definitions and lists of words arranged for the convenience of solvers. Curiously, however, few books have any advice on how to solve crossword puzzles, and almost none tell you how to compose them. The main topics of our book are the solving and composing of crosswords.

You don't have to be an Oxford scholar to solve or compose puzzles. Obviously, a large vocabulary and familiarity with languages help—wit is also a tool of the trade. But these are not prerequisites, they are easily and speedily developed with practice.

Our book focuses on the conventional American crossword puzzle as found in magazines and most daily and Sunday newspapers. We also discuss other forms of crossword puzzles, such as the typical British cryptic crossword, with its initially indecipherable definitions; the diagramless puzzle, a very satisfying type for the solver, and not nearly so difficult as it appears at first; and the acrostic puzzle.

We have divided our book into three independent sections. The first part is about the history of crossword puzzles and the people who were prominent in that history. The next part tells you how to solve crossword puzzles, but as a *solver*, you should also read the following part on composition. An insight into the composer's thoughts can help you solve puzzles.

We hope that the chapters on composition will persuade you to try your own hand at our emotionally most rewarding hobby. Therefore, we have included a chapter devoted to considerations of marketing puzzles.

To spice our *chef d'oeuvre*, we have included an appendix on non-English puzzles. Finally, although we define the words that make up our puzzlers' jargon as they are introduced, we have included a glossary.

Titles of puzzles appear in the text capitalized and in quotation marks: "WIRE SERVICE." Examples of definitions appear in quotation marks: "Three-toed sloths." Words or phrases used as examples of answers are capitalized and not in quotation marks: CURRENT EVENTS. Terms found in the glossary are *italicized* when they first appear in the text.

When we are not apuzzling, we work as computer scientists. We are often asked what role the computer will play in composing tomorrow's crosswords. A program[1] has been written which, its author claims, produces German crossword puzzles as good as those that people create, within the constraints of a small (10,000-word) vocabulary and small puzzle size. Projects[2] based on puzzles in English have not been so ambitious. In practice, phrases, abbreviations, foreign words, proper nouns, etc., enlarge a human composer's vocabulary far beyond the largest computer's ability to cope with the resulting possibilities for compositions. When computers can make puzzle composers obsolete, they will already have wrought far more interesting changes to our world.

A final point: the Italian word for crossword puzzle is *cruciverba*, whence the title of our

1. Volume

ꓘꓤOⱲ 'ƎⱮOꓕ 'SꓵꓒO 'ꓘOOꓭ

---

[1]O. Feger, "Program for Constructing Crossword Puzzles," (*Ein Programm zur Konstruktion von Kreuzworträtseln*), *Angewandte Informatik*, 1975 5, Pages 189-195.

[2]H.A. Bauer, "A Program to Solve Crossword Puzzles," Master's Thesis, Northwestern University, Evanston, Illinois, 1973.

L. J. Mazlack, "Machine Selection of Elements in Crossword Puzzles: An Application of Computational Linguistics," *SIAM Journal of Computing,* **5,** March 1976, Pages 51-72.

E. S. Spiegelthal, "Redundancy Exploitation in the Computer Construction of Double Crostics," *Proceedings of the Eastern Joint Computer Conference*, 1960, Pages 39-56.

P. W. Williams and D. Woodhead, "Computer-assisted Analysis of Cryptic Crosswords," *Computer Journal*, 22 1, 1979, Pages 67-70.

D. Woodhead, "Computer Aids to the Solution of Cryptic Crossword Puzzles," Third Year Project Report, UMIST.

Acknowledgments

We are grateful to Nina Kurzban and Peggy Rosen for reading and commenting forcefully on the first draft of our book, to Will Weng for a critical reading of the second draft, and to Robert Malstrom for his valuable comments. We thank Sharon Jacobson and Nina Kurzban for typing and retyping.

We also thank:

The *St. Louis Post-Dispatch*, for permission to reprint Arthur Wynne's first "word-cross" puzzle, originally published December 21, 1913, in the *New York World,*

Simon and Schuster, for permission to reprint the opening puzzle in *The Cross Word Puzzle Book*, Copyright 1924 by Plaza Publishing Co., renewed 1952 by Simon and Schuster, a Division of Gulf & Western Corporation, and

Saturday Review, for permission to reprint Double-Crostic #1, © *Saturday Review*, 1934. All rights reserved.

Contents

THE COMPLEAT
CRUCIVERBALIST

I
BACKGROUND

1
History of Cruciverbalism

In the beginning was the Word.—John 1:1

CROSSWORD PUZZLES

Games, puzzles, and geometric arrangements involving letters and words have amused people ever since the beginnings of written language. Ancestral forms of the crossword puzzles we enjoy today existed more than 2000 years ago.

Magic squares and other shapes in which numbers are arranged in special ways—to produce a constant sum when rows or columns are added, for instance—were well known in ancient times. The oldest known word square, a derivative of the magic square using letters instead of numbers, dates back to the first century A.D.:

```
R  O  T  A  S
O  P  E  R  A
T  E  N  E  T
A  R  E  P  O
S  A  T  O  R
```

This square can be read row by row, column by column, forward or backward. The Latin words have been translated as, "Arepo, the sower, watches over his works," which has been interpreted to mean, "God watches over the universe."

The Sator Square, as this arrangement is known, was first discovered in England in 1868, in a church built by the Romans in about A.D. 300. Theologians debated its religious significance for years. Then, about 70 years later, it was discovered among the ruins at Pompeii. Since this particular inscription must have been made before the eruption of

3

Vesuvius in A.D. 79, all the religious theories had to be discarded. In the first place, Christianity was not common in that region at that time. In the second place, and of overriding importance, much of the Christian symbolism that had been attributed to the square had not yet come into use. No one today knows for sure if the Sator Square had any significance at all.

Another arrangement of letters is not so much a puzzle as an artistic curiosity. The "stele of Moschion," an engraving in alabaster created about A.D. 300, is a square grid with 39 small squares on each side. Each small square contains a single Greek letter. Beginning at the center of the grid, and progressing outwards in many ways, one can make out the inscription, "Moschion to Osiris, for the treatment that cured his foot."

In the mid-1800s one form of entertainment—the arrangement of letters into pleasing shapes and word squares—merged with another entertainment, the riddle or conundrum. Magazines began publishing "clues" which, if solved, led to word squares. Through most of the Victorian age, puzzles involving crossing words usually produced squares, although there were some stepladder- and diamond-shaped constructions in which the horizontal words were not the same as the vertical words.

Late in 1913, Arthur Wynne, who composed a page of puzzles every week for the Sunday *New York World,* decided to create something different from his usual fare of rebuses, anagrams, word squares, and riddles. The new puzzle, which he called a "word-cross," appeared December 21, 1913, and it was a sensation.

Mr. Wynne constructed another "word-cross" puzzle for the following Sunday paper, and, to the irritation of the typographers, fans clamored for more. Readers began sending their own compositions at the rate of about one a day.

The Sunday *World* was the only publisher of crossword puzzles for about ten years. The newspaper's editors played down the feature by setting the puzzle in the smallest available typeface, obviously not understanding how popular it had become.

In 1924, Dick Simon and Max Schuster began the business of publishing crossword puzzle books. Legend has it they got the idea as a result of a casual conversation in which they heard that one of Simon's cousins enjoyed the puzzles in the paper very much and wanted more. Each of the three puzzle editors at the *World* was offered $25 advance against royalties to do a little moonlighting and piece together a book. Margaret Petherbridge (who became Margaret Farrar when she married in

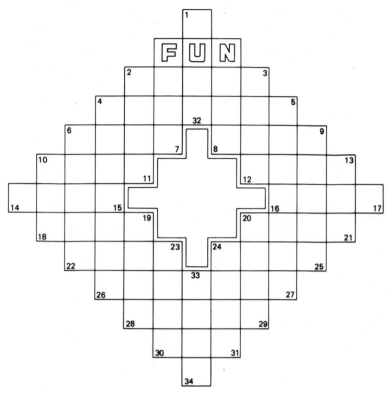

2-3.   What bargain hunters enjoy.
4-5.   A written acknowledgment.
18-19. What this puzzle is.
22-23. An animal of prey.
26-27. The close of a day.
28-29. To elude.
30-31. The plural of is.
8-9.   To cultivate.
12-13. A bar of wood or iron.
16-17. What artists learn to do.
20-21. Fastened.
24-25. Found on the seashore.
10-18. The fiber of the gomuti palm.
6-22.   What we all should be.

6-7.   Such and nothing more.
10-11. A bird.
14-15. Opposed to less.
4-26.   A day dream.
2-11.   A talon.
19-28. A pigeon.
F-7.   Part of your head.
23-30. A river in Russia.
1-32.   To govern.
33-34. An aromatic plant.
N-8.   A fist.
24-31. To agree with.
3-12.   Part of a ship.
20-29. One.
5-27.   Exchanging.
9-25.   To sink in mud.
13-21. A boy.

Figure 1-1   Arthur Wynne's first "word-cross" puzzle.

A SOFT BEGINNING
By Gregorian

The two long central words, if solved at once, will give sufficient clues to permit of rapid solution. But should these prove elusive, surely such definitions as 9 horizontal and 29 vertical offer no difficulties. Three-letter words meaning respectively "aged" and "sorrowful" should hold few terrors for the beginner.

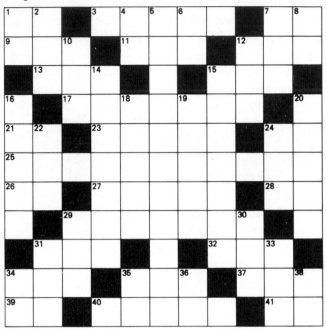

Figure 1-2   The first puzzle in the first puzzle book.

HORIZONTAL

1 Pronoun
3 Albumin from castor-oil bean
7 Exist
9 Aged
11 Negative
12 Incite, hasten
13 Remote
15 Obstruction
17 Bivalves
21 Father
23 Tree
24 River in Italy
25 Owners
26 Printer's measure
27 Tree
28 Personal pronoun
29 Legislative bodies
31 Compact mass
32 Moved rapidly
34 Walk about
35 Toss
37 Small child
39 Upon
40 Small openings
41 Act

VERTICAL

1 Exclamation
2 Fairy
4 Preposition
5 Plotter
6 Pronoun
7 Express generally
8 Pronoun
10 Obstruct
12 Owns
14 Disarranged
15 Voluble talkativeness
16 Above
18 The bow of Vishnu
19 Choose
20 Assumed an attitude
22 Limb
24 Peer
29 Sorrowful
30 Rested
31 Pale
33 Incline the head
34 Move
35 Behold
36 Exist
38 Preposition

1926), Prosper Buranelli, and F. Gregory Hartswick collected and prepared 50 puzzles which were released in an edition of 3600 copies. Hartswick composed the first puzzle in the book, disguising his authorship by the pseudonym "Gregorian." Simon and Schuster were concerned that they might be hooted out of the publishing business after only a few months in it, and so, when the book was published on April 10, 1924, it carried the name "Plaza Publishing Company" on the title page. "Plaza" was the telephone exchange at Simon and Schuster's offices.

The first printing of *The Cross Word Puzzle Book* sold out quickly. Simon and Schuster came out from behind the "Plaza" facade, and by the end of 1924 the company was represented on the best-seller list by four puzzle books. For good luck and for sentimental reasons the name "Plaza" remained on the title page of the puzzle books for a number of years. Simon and Schuster, success assured, were able to expand into other publishing avenues. The three co-editors continued to compile puzzle books, to the delight of millions of eager buyers.

On May 18, 1924, some 300 people met in New York City and founded the Crossword Puzzlers' Association of America. Joseph E. Austrian was elected president.

Crossword puzzles quickly became one of the most popular amusements of the time. Never before had a fad received such extensive news coverage. Between November 17 and December 23, 1924, the *New York Times* published over 20 articles and editorials related to crossword puzzles. The paper continued to run articles and editorial comments from time to time for the next 5 years. The material in the remainder of this section is drawn primarily from items that appeared in the *Times*. (The dates we mention are dates of publication, and not necessarily those of the actual events.)

On November 17, 1924, the *Times* declared in an editorial that crossword puzzles were "scarcely removed from the form of temporary madness that made so many people pay enormous sums for mah jong sets." Another editorial four days later continued the ridicule.

In an article published November 24 the same year, Johns Hopkins University in Baltimore speculated that an artifact called the "Phaestus Disk" could have been a forerunner of modern word puzzles. This terra cotta disk, apparently of Cretan origin and perhaps dating from 2000 B.C., was on display in the Johns Hopkins Archeological Museum. It was described as having untranslated symbols arranged in a spiral. The symbols may have made sense when read working outward from the center, or inward from the rim.

A week later, two Princeton University professors issued challenges to their respective classes. Warner Fite, a professor of Logic, offered a prize for a successfully compiled crossword puzzle in which a single set of definitions would lead to two completely different, yet equally correct sets of answers for a single diagram. No one claimed the prize.[1] A professor of English, Robert Root, made the excellent suggestion that it would be valuable to establish an English vocabulary course using crossword puzzles as text material.

On December 1, 1924, it was reported that George McElveen, a Baptist preacher in Pittsburgh, had stayed up all night "working out his combinations" for a crossword puzzle, the solution to which was the text for his next sermon. The church overflowed with puzzle fans the following Sunday. The congregation solved the puzzle, which was set up on a large blackboard at the front of the church, before Reverend McElveen delivered the sermon.

While Reverend McElveen was hard at work using his crossword puzzle to entice people to church, another man came to regret his encounter with a puzzle. W. Nathan became engrossed in a puzzle book while dining at a New York restaurant. Armed with a dictionary, and with kibitzers looking over his shoulder, he refused to leave his table at closing time. He was finally arrested for disturbing the peace.

In a profile published December 2, 1924, the *Times* called Fanny Goldner the city's oldest puzzle fan. The 103-year-old woman became interested in puzzles when an attendant at her nursing home compiled one in Yiddish. The *Times* did not report whether English or Hebrew letters were used.

Nine days later, a woman in Cleveland was granted a divorce from a puzzle addict. In court she testified, "Morning, noon, and night, it is crossword puzzles."

The United States Department of Agriculture, bowing under the weight of numerous requests from puzzle-solvers, released an announcement on December 12, revealing the name of the Roman goddess of agriculture— Ops. The announcement went on to say that the department was in no way setting a precedent, either for itself or for any other governmental body, by giving out such information.

---

[1] Several compilers of cryptic crossword puzzles have achieved *double-entendre*. We discuss later in this book the differences between cryptic and conventional crossword puzzles that facilitate accomplishment of the feat in cryptic crossword puzzles.

The Baltimore & Ohio Railroad announced that it would supply dictionaries in the club cars for passenger convenience, initially on the main rail lines, and probably eventually on the branch lines as well.

On December 20, 1924, two inmates in a Pittsburgh jail got into a fight. They had decided to bring a crossword puzzle book to pass the time while they did time. When they came to a four-letter word defined as "Place of punishment," with the letters __ELL filled in, they could not resolve the choice, CELL or HELL, without resorting to fisticuffs.

Times articles over the next several days commented on the increased sale of dictionaires. The Los Angeles Public Library established a five minute limit on the use of a dictionary. In an editorial, the *New York Times* commented, "The only comfort of non-puzzlers is that the paper on which the sacred documents are printed cannot endure through the ages ... no one has yet seen fit to engrave his favorite puzzle on his headstone."

Late in the year, a "wild-eyed mob" besieged the Carnegie Library in Pittsburgh, demanding that the curator tell them a word of seven letters meaning, "a bird of the suborder of *eleutherodactyli oscines*." After some reflection, the curator responded "sparrow"—which was hardly the extinct relative of the pterodactyl the crowd thought it was after.

The first few days of 1925 made it clear that the fad was not dying out. In Paris, it was reported, American women were infatuated with hosiery imprinted with black and white squares in random patterns. The Parisian women, needless to say, pronounced the fashion "hideous." At about the same time, an American designer produced a line of clothes made up from material depicting puzzle fragments. A book given away with each purchase contained the complete set of puzzles and definitions. Anyone answering all the puzzles in the book was thereafter entitled to a discount on other dresses in the line. (No one ever reported any difficulties trying to solve a puzzle while the dress was occupied.)

Carnegie Library in Pittsburgh announced, on January 4, 1925, that it had no books of puzzles in the library, and furthermore, that it had no intention of acquiring any, as "they're not literature."

The following day Yale beat Wellesley in a crossword-puzzle solving contest that had been arranged as a benefit for Bryn Mawr.

On January 6, 1925, the *New York Times* reported that a group of puzzle enthusiasts had to be reprimanded in a New York City courtroom because they had become so involved with their collective efforts that they failed to notice the arrival of the judge. It turned out that one of the puzzle-doers was a defendant who was in court for the second time because he ignored a fine imposed the week before. His excuse was that he had been sidetracked by a puzzle.

An article appearing January 13, 1925, reported that Queen Mary and some of her companions had taken time out from other activities to try solving crossword puzzles. In an editorial the next day the *New York Times* commented: "Royalty in ages past has been worse employed more than once." The paper went on to say that Queen Mary's participation in puzzling, and similar popular activities by other rulers, "humanizes royalty."

On January 21, the *Times* reported that a newspaper called the *Daily Graphic*, which offered prizes for successful puzzle solving, was seeking an injunction barring another paper, the *Bronx Home News*, from publishing the answers. The *Home News* claimed during its defense that while the puzzles may have been copyrighted, the answers were not.

Crossword puzzles really "arrived" on January 29, 1925, with an item on page 1 of the *New York Times*. W. R. Baker, President of the British Optical Association, warned of headaches due to eyestrain caused by the combination of the small type used for puzzles and the need to shift the eyes and refocus rapidly when solving puzzles.

On February 1, the *New York Times* conceded, "the almost universal hobby of the moment is the crossword puzzle." However, the editorial went on to observe that such activity serves "no useful purpose whatever."

The following week, the *Times* Sunday Magazine featured a biography of Roget, calling him "the patron saint of crossworders."

On February 15, the Associated Press reported that Paris, and, indeed, all of mainland Europe had taken to crosswords. Actually, the Belgian paper *Le Soir* began offering puzzles a week before any of the Parisian papers. The papers awarded prizes to successful solvers, but there was trouble under the lottery laws and the police seized some 6000 submitted solutions.

The next day brought news that a library in Dulwich, England, had taken to blotting out the puzzles in the papers because addicts were keeping the papers from the other readers. Two days later, Wimbledon Library removed all "volumes of lexicography" from the shelves because of damage.

On February 22, it was reported that the Foreign Language Information

Service, an organization whose purpose was to help immigrants learn English, was publishing crossword puzzles, with definitions in 16 different languages and answers in English. A list of some 4000 "most needed" words, augmented by names of historically important Americans, supplied the answers.

On the same day, the *New York Times* reported that the Prime Minister of Britain, Stanley Baldwin, had relaxed by solving a puzzle, with the help of M. Panileve, the Premier of France, and M. Briand, the French Foreign Minister.

The Chicago Department of Health got into the act with an announcement that, in their view, "crossworditis" was beneficial to health and happiness. (They undoubtedly meant "crosswordosis.") The *Times* gave this item a place on page 1 on March 9.

In March, the *New Republic* concluded that crosswords were not educational, being but "bad exercise for writers and speakers." In an editorial on March 10, the *Times* commented that "the craze is evidently dying out fast," and that crosswords were "going the way of mah jong."

In a letter published a week later, a Mr. Brockelbank rebutted the *Times*, arguing that mah jong was "doomed from the start," being too much based on luck.

In June, a trade paper for undertakers carried a crossword puzzle featuring scientific and technical terms dealing with funeral directing and embalming.

On Broadway, the show *Tell Me More!* (book by Fred Thompson and William K. Wells, music by George Gershwin, lyrics by B. G. DeSylva and Ira Gershwin) contained this snapper: "I hope you're stranded on a desert isle with a crossword puzzle and without a dictionary." Another show, *Puzzles of 1925* (by Elsie Janis), went even further, with a skit depicting puzzle addicts as patients in a sanitorium.

The phrase "Long live Otto," supporting nationalistic calls to put Archduke Otto on the Hungarian throne, cropped up in a puzzle in a Hungarian paper in October 1925. The dictatorial government of Admiral Horthy immediately began censoring the puzzles.

The year 1925 ended on an unhappy note, so far as news pertaining to crossword puzzles is concerned. Theodore Koerner, a 27-year-old employee of the New York Telephone Company, shot and wounded his wife because she refused to help him solve a crossword puzzle. He then killed himself.

The year 1926 brought more unhappy news. A Budapest waiter named Julius Antar committed suicide. He explained why in a crossword puzzle which, alas, the police were unable to solve.

At the February 1927 convention of the National Puzzlers' League, Secretary Lewis Trent said that crossword puzzles had no place in the life of a "true puzzler." According to Mr. Trent, pastimes such as anagrams, enigmas, and rebuses deserved more attention. At that convention, incidentally, William Grossman presented what was called "the perfect anagram." The conventioneers sat enthralled as the words THEY SEE were written on a blackboard, then rearranged to form THE EYES.

Picking up on Secretary Trent's remarks, the *Times* printed an editorial on February 23, 1927 declaring the "crossword epidemic" to be over. The paper noted the popularity of new amusements, cryptograms and anagrams.

The London *Times* introduced a weekly crossword puzzle on January 23, 1930. The *Daily Telegraph*, a rival newspaper, reacted by running an advertisement in the London *Times* the very next day. The ad, which featured a crossword puzzle, exhorted *Times* readers to buy the *Daily Telegraph* if they wanted a puzzle every day. The *Times* received many letters asking that they make the crossword a daily feature. They did so on February 1, 1930. The *New York Times* editorialized that crossword puzzling was "plainly past its prime in the U.S.," and wondered why the London *Times* had bothered to start a puzzle feature.

The first crossword puzzles printed in British papers were similar to those published in America. Diagrams looked very much like those seen here, and composers in England originally used straightforward definitions. By 1930, however, misleading, tricky clues were gaining popularity in England. In an editorial printed February 15, 1930, entitled "It presupposes a University education," the *New York Times* wrote that the London *Times* was making a mistake by allowing humor and whimsy into the puzzle definitions. As an example the *New York Times* cited the clue "Sounds like a curious song." The answer was ODDITY, which sounds like ODD DITTY, a "curious song." This "may be imagination or anagrams or Badminton or something, but it's not crossword puzzling," said the *Times*.

Puzzles containing humorous definitions also acquired a following in America. Ted Shane, Albert Morehead, and Jack Luzzatto were among the first American constructors to create crossword puzzles that, as *Judge* magazine once said, were "not edited in conformity with any rules whatever," as long as the definitions were "ambidextrous and witty."

The cryptic puzzles published in England went beyond "ambidextrous and witty." Because of the deviousness of the puzzles, and because people are naturally drawn to competition, British puzzle fans took to writing letters to the newspapers to congratulate themselves on the speed with which they could solve the puzzles. According to the *Guinness Book of World Records*, Roy Dean solved a puzzle in less than four minutes. His achievement was remarkable in that it occurred under extreme pressure—the London *Times* contest conducted in the BBC studios on December 19, 1970. A woman in Fiji established a perverse record when she notified the London *Times* in May 1966 that she had just completed puzzle #673, published in April 1932.

British puzzle fans tried to deduce the identity of the compiler(s) based on recurring clues, themes, and technical or literary references. The first puzzle compiler for the London *Times* was a Suffolk farmer named Adrian Bell. A relative recommended him to the paper. He had never even solved a puzzle before being hired as a constructor.

The Nation has carried a cryptic puzzle since 1943. Upon the death of the magazine's first composer, its readers chose Frank Lewis over another aspirant on the basis of 12 puzzles published anonymously.

The *New York Times* finally joined in. The paper hired Margaret Farrar to be puzzle editor, and on February 15, 1942 the Sunday Magazine carried a large (23 squares by 23 squares, commonly written as "23 x 23") crossword puzzle of "topical interest." A small (15 x 15) humorous puzzle titled "Riddle Me This," contributed by one "Anna Gram,"[2] accompanied the large puzzle. An announcement on the same page invited free-lance contributions. The *Times* began offering a daily crossword puzzle in 1950. They gave it prominent space on the Book Page, where it is found today.

ACROSTIC PUZZLES

Acrostic Puzzles have two ancestors, the acrostic and the anagram.

Acrostics

The word "acrostic" comes from the Greek roots *akros*, "extreme," and *stikhos*, "line of verse." Thus, an acrostic is a verse or set of lines in which the first letters spell something significant.

---

[2] "Anna Gram" has been used as a pseudonym, or *nom de puzzle*, to conceal the identities of several puzzle constructors, including Margaret Farrar herself.

It is likely that the early bards and balladeers used acrostic devices as memory aids to help in recalling verses of epic poems and songs. Several specimens of acrostics occur in the original Hebrew scriptures. The best known is Psalm 119: in Hebrew the first verse begins with the letter *aleph*, the second with the letter *beth,* and so on through the Hebrew alphabet. The acrostic is lost in translation, but many modern bibles use the Hebrew letters to mark off the separate verses.

The fish as a symbol for Christ remains as a vestige of a Greek acrostic. The Greek word for "fish" is ιχθυς, and the acrostic runs as follows:

$$Ιησους—Jesus$$
$$Χριστος—Christ,$$
$$Θεου—of God,$$
$$Υιος—Son,$$
$$Σωτηρ—Savior.$$

According to Cicero, the Sibyls, ten women who were inspired with prophetic power by the god Apollo, often wrote their oracles in acrostic form. Other mystical claims and writings through the years were based on acrostics. But acrostics never took hold as a general form of amusement, perhaps because they represent no puzzle. They are, after all, simply an arrangement of letters.

As an art form, acrostics came into some favor toward the end of the 17th century. An 1875 book titled *Gleanings for the Curious from the Harvest-Fields of Literature, a Melange of Excerptia*, collected (or "collated," as the title page puts it) by C. C. Bombaugh, contains this uncredited acrostic poem on the poet Wordsworth:

Wandering, through many a year, 'mongst Cumbria's hills,
O 'er her wild fells, sweet vales, and sunny lakes,
R ich stores of thought thy musing mind distils,
D ay-dreams of poesy thy soul awakes:—
S uch was thy life—a poet's life, I ween;
W orshipper thou of Nature! every scene
O f beauty stirred by thy fancy's deeper mood,
R eflection calmed the current of thy blood:
T hus in the wide "excursion" of thy mind,
H igh thought in *words* of *worth* we still may find.

Of course, many writers used the acrostic and related devices to excess. Here, from the same book, is part of a title page "for a book of extracts from many authors":

Astonishing Anthology from Attractive Authors.
Broken Bits from Bulky Brains.
Choice Chunks from Chaucer to Channing.

•

•

•

Xcellent Xtracts Xactly Xpressed.
Yawnings and Yearnings for Youthful Yankees.
Zeal and Zest from Zoroaster to Zimmerman.

This example is properly called a *pangrammatic* ("containing all letters") or an alphabetic alliteration. Like most forays into this arena, it becomes more than a little strained at the letter "X."

Today the acrostic appears in decline as an art form. Except for acrostic puzzles as described in this book, its most common appearance is on political billboards, where the letters in a candidate's name are used as the initial letters of words in a list of praiseworthy attributes.

Anagrams

The second ancestor of the acrostic puzzle, the anagram, also arose in antiquity. The word comes from the Greek roots *ana*, "back, or reversed," and *gramma*, "letter" (or *grammos*, "line"). An anagram is a rearrangement of the letters in a word or phrase to produce a new word or phrase. For example, "astronomers" can be rearranged to form "moonstarers" or "no more stars."

A Greek writer named Lycophron, who lived during the fourth century before Christ, may have originated the oldest surviving anagrams. His poem *Cassandra*, on the fall of Troy, contains flattering anagrams on the names of the reigning Egyptian king and queen.

Soothsayers, oracles, and prophets used anagrams as one source for their advice. They labored to rearrange the letters in names, trying to produce apt phrases. Both supporters of Martin Luther and those opposed to his doctrines composed anagrams on his name in German and in Latin to make their points. *Martin Luther* became *lehrt in Armut* ("He teaches in poverty"). *Martinus Luterus* became both *vir multa struens* ("the man who builds up much") and *ter matris vulnus* ("He wounded the mother [church] three times").

In the 1800s the phrase "Govern, clever lad" honored Grover Cleveland. More recently, someone formed the descriptive phrase "now has a

1	2	3	■	4	5	6	■	7	8	■	9	10	11	■
12	13	14	■	15	16	17	■	18	19	20	21	■	22	23
24	25	26	27	28	29	■	30	31	32	33	34	■	35	36
■	37	38	39	■	40	41	42	43	■	44	45	46	47	48
■	49	50	51	52	53	■	54	55	56	■	57	58	59	60
61	62	■	63	64	65	66	■	67	68	69	70	71	■	72
73	■	74	75	76	■	77	78	■	79	80	81	■	82	83
84	■	85	86	87	88	89	■	90	91	92	93	94	95	■
96	97	■	98	99	100	101	102	103	■	104	105	106	107	108
109	■	110	111	112	113	■	114	115	116	117	■	118	119	■
120	121	122	123	■	124	125	126	■	127	128	129	130	■	131
132	133	■	134	135	136	137	138	139	■	140	141	■	142	143
144	145	■	146	147	■	148	149	150	151	152	153	■	154	155
■	156	157	158	159	■	160	161	■	162	163	164	165	■	166
167	168	■	169	170	171	■	172	173	■	174	175	176	177	178

DIRECTIONS

To solve this puzzle, you must guess twenty-five words, the definitions of which are given in the column headed DEFINITIONS. The letters in each word to be guessed are numbered (these numbers appear at the beginning of each definition) and you are thereby able to tell how many letters are in the required word. When you have guessed a word each letter is to be written in the correspondingly numbered square on the puzzle diagram. When the squares are all filled in you will find (by reading from left to right) a quotation from a famous author. Reading up and down, the letters mean nothing! The black squares indicate ends of words; therefore words do not necessarily end at the right side of the diagram.

Either before (preferably) or after placing the letters in their squares you should write the words you have guessed on the blank lines which appear to the right in the column headed WORDS. The initial letters of this list of words spell the name of the author and the title of the piece from which the quotation has been taken.

Figure 1-3   Double-Crostic #1.

NOTICE

This is the first of a series of ingenious literary puzzles invented by Elizabeth S. Kingsley for *The Saturday Review*. A new puzzle will be published each week, and the answer to the previous puzzle will appear regularly in this space. Let us know if the DIRECTIONS are clear. And after you have solved several of the puzzles we should like to know whether you think them too hard or too easy— our DEFINITIONS will be governed accordingly! Write to THE PUZZLE EDITOR, THE SATURDAY REVIEW, 25 WEST 45TH STREET, NEW YORK CITY.

DEFINITIONS

WORDS

I. 1-14-23-50-95. A perfume of roses.

I. _____

II. 145-6-28-90-137. Child's game played with cards and numbers.

II. _____

III. 97-8-79-146-98-61-75-77-76-32-27-19-133. Light as a feather.

III. _____

IV. 80-85-60-113-51-58-48. Held in high esteem; worshipped.

IV. _____

V. 81-172-31-84-24-176-65-89. Insubstantial.

V. _____

VI. 112-45-114-164-149-173-142-36. The business section of a city.

VI. _____

VII. 144-102-2-63. Material for bandages.

VII. _____

VIII. 37-4-66-82-110-116-62. Upholstered backless seat.

VIII. _____

IX. 100-106-33-5-122-41-138-69-83-13-162-127. A Russian pianist.

IX. _____

X. 40-59-52-25. A drupe with a single seed.

X. _____

XI. 135-175-3-73. Movement of the ocean.

XI. _____

XII. 130-43-129-107-111-55-139-47. To alienate.

XII. _____

XIII. 15-121-92-136-101-39. A mighty hunter.

XIII. _____

XIV. 167-9-140-46-105. Artless; simple.

XIV. _____

XV. 119-54-104-17-153-34. Hebrew God.

XV. _____

XVI. 134-63-128-168-16-30. Flat, dark image.

XVI. _____

XVII. 155-125-78-148-143-165-158-56. Prejudiced (compound).

XVII. _____

XVIII. 12-96-120-11-7-170-150-21-68-174. Significant, unusual.

XVIII. _____

XIX. 97-141-171-161-67-20-10-126. Not propitious.

XIX. _____

XX. 177-99-152-163-108-115. Member of the tribe of Levi.

XX. _____

XXI. 42-88-26-159-49-91. Doodle dandy.

XXI. _____

XXII. 22-71-151-118-131-147-38-94-160-29. Watchword (Bibl.).

XXII. _____

XXIII. 109-86-132-124-72-117-123-178. Uttered a harsh sound.

XXIII. _____

XXIV. 157-44-93-53-166-18-35-103. Forceful.

XXIV. _____

XXV. 156-154-74-169-70-57. To stop the flow.

XXV. _____

wide, ever-delighted grin" from the letters in the words "General Dwight David Eisenhower."

The anagram remains a popular entertainment, much more so than the acrostic. This is undoubtedly due to the fact that more skill is needed to create an anagram, especially an apt one. Indeed, much of the significance attributed to the Sator Square came from the many anagrams composed from its letters. In 1925, for instance, a Reverend Hicks noted that SATOR OPERA TENET was an anagram of PATER NOSTER A ET O. A ET O was taken to mean "Alpha and Omega," or, "the Beginning and the End."

Anagrams play a large part in the clues for cryptic crossword puzzles and humorous puzzles such as "Puns and Anagrams." Occasionally some outstanding anagrams crop up in conventional crossword puzzles. Will Shortz, who is the only person known to hold a degree in Enigmatology (the study of puzzles and games), once presented "It's now seen live" as the definition for TELEVISION NEWS.

Invention of the Modern Acrostic Puzzle

In the early 1930s Mrs. Elizabeth Kingsley returned to her alma mater, Wellesley College, for a class reunion. The undergraduates' taste in literature displeased her so much that she set out to devise a puzzle to heighten appreciation by, as she later noted, "reviewing classical English and American poet and prose masters." The first Double-Crostic was published by *The Saturday Review of Literature* on March 31, 1934. The magazine invited solvers to make suggestions to improve the puzzle—for instance, by making the clues harder or easier—and published letters concerning the puzzle for some weeks.

In an acrostic puzzle the notions of acrostics and anagrams are merged together with definitions. The writer of an acrostic puzzle rearranges the letters in an excerpt from some published work to form a series of words. The solver must deduce the words from definitions. The series of words is an acrostic. The first letters of the words, taken in order, spell something—usually the name of the author of the passage and the title of the work from which the passage was taken. (In some magazines or syndicated puzzles the acrostic spells the name of a person or place that is the subject of the quotation.)

Today, millions of puzzle solvers enjoy the special challenge acrostic puzzles provide.

OTHER FORMS

Just as crosswords and acrostic puzzles descended from earlier amusements, so too have new puzzle forms arisen from crosswords and acrostic puzzles. The names for the types of puzzles differ from publisher to publisher. Some of the popular ones are skeleton puzzles, in which words must be chosen from a list and placed in open interlocking patterns; fill-ins, in which words must be chosen from a list and placed in crossword puzzle patterns; and cross-number puzzles, in which digits are entered in crossword puzzle patterns so as to add to supplied sums.

The *Reporter,* an American magazine published from 1949 to 1968, carried what may be the ultimate form of crossword puzzle. The "Acrostickler," composed by Henry Allen, had diagrams and clues similar to cryptic crossword puzzles. The unchecked letters in the diagram recombined to form words in an acrostic yielding the name of some prominent person. A few answers in the diagram pertained to that person in some way, perhaps consisting of the person's birthplace, profession, or the like.

When the *Reporter* ceased publication, *Harper's Monthly* picked up the Acrostickler, but they dropped it at the end of 1969. It may simply have been too extreme to survive.

2
Who's Who of Puzzledom

These were honored in their generations, and were the glory of the times—Ecclesiasticus

MARGARET PETHERBRIDGE FARRAR

In the first *Cross Word Puzzle Book* Margaret Petherbridge called herself the "unwilling" puzzle editor of the *New York World*. The *World* had assigned Miss Petherbridge, a Smith College graduate, to select the puzzle that would appear in the daily paper. Her method was to pick a "good-looking" one and send it off to be set in type. When Franklin P. Adams carped, in his popular "Conning Tower" column, about typographical errors, missing definitions, and other mistakes in the puzzles, Margaret decided to treat the puzzles more seriously.

The success of the Simon and Schuster puzzle books firmly established Mrs. Farrar as America's preeminent editor of crossword puzzles. The *New York Times* hired her to be puzzle editor when the paper began offering a puzzle feature in 1942. Mrs. Farrar retired from the *Times* in 1969. She remains active in puzzling, however, and after 57 years she still treats puzzles seriously. The Simon and Schuster books now number well over 100 under her guiding hand. She edits collections for Pocket Book publications and keeps an eye on books of reprints of *Times* puzzles. She still samples the daily *Times* crossword, but frequently does not take the time to finish it.

Mrs. Farrar has held one rule inviolable throughout her long career: the solver must enjoy working the puzzle. To this end, Mrs. Farrar strictly prohibits anything that might be considered to be in poor taste. She once requested revision of a puzzle containing the phrase BLOOD TESTS among several thematic answers related to weddings and marriage. The substitution, ELOPEMENTS, satisfied her, and she published the puzzle one June Sunday.

Mrs. Farrar remembers several crosswords particularly well. One of her favorites was "YKCOWREBBAJ," which proved, she said later, that "some people managed to grow up without knowledge of *Alice in Wonderland*." (The title of the puzzle is the word "Jabberwocky" in reverse. The composer of the puzzle, Frances Hansen, specializes today in puzzles incorporating original humorous poetry.)

Another of Mrs. Farrar's favorite puzzles was composed by J. Arensberg and H. Ettenson. "FIGURES OF SPEECH" contained outrageous examples of different figures of speech and their technical names.

It is impossible to count the people who owe thanks to Mrs. Farrar for hours of entertainment. It is almost impossible to count the puzzle constructors she has helped and encouraged. She is the Queen of Puzzledom.

WILL WENG

Will Weng, who succeeded Mrs. Farrar at the *New York Times*, was born in Terre Haute, Indiana. He planned to follow his father and two sisters and become an educator, but his father pushed him into journalism. Mr. Weng graduated from the Columbia University School of Journalism having learned how to "report fires and write editorials," and joined the *Times* as a reporter. He recalls that his first assignment was to cover a swimming race around Manhattan Island. The promoter skipped and the winners were never paid.

Mr. Weng eventually became head of the city desk, in charge of editing other reporters' stories and writing headlines. In his spare time, he contributed some puzzles to the *Times* Sunday Magazine. For that reason, and because he "happened to be handy," the *Times* selected him to be Puzzle Editor when Mrs. Farrar retired.

Mr. Weng remembers that on about the third day the *Times* had been running their new daily puzzle, the printers somehow omitted it. When they discovered the error partway through the press run there was a big to-do. The presses were stopped to insert the puzzle for the rest of the edition.

During his reign at the *Times* Mr. Weng brought a different style of puzzle into vogue. He had always enjoyed puns, and he accepted them in greater numbers than they had ever been accepted before. In one of Mr. Weng's own compositions the definition "Is your doctor influential?" led to the answer NO, BUT MY DENTIST HAS A PULL.

During his editorship Mr. Weng was forced on several occasions to explain the gimmicks in the puzzles to bewildered letter-writers. William Lutwiniak supplied a puzzle with the definition "AVI." The answer turned out to be THE CENTER OF GRAVITY. (Notice the letters in the middle of the word "gravity.") The same puzzle contained "EL," the BOTTOM OF THE BARREL, and "OA," the MIDDLE OF THE ROAD. The puzzle's apt title was "SPOT ANNOUNCEMENTS."

In another remarkable construction, "SQUARELY FIGURED," by A. J. Santora, the gimmick was that digits were to be entered in the diagram, and sometimes two or three digits in a single square—but what a puzzle! Each occurrence of digits concided with a square that already contained those digits as a natural result of numbering the diagram. At 76 Down, for instance, the answer was 76 TROMBONES. Both digits fit in a single square. The crossing answer was 76ERS, referring to the Philadelphia basketball team.

Mr. Weng allowed other experiments, including ideas taken from rebus puzzles. He accepted compositions in which symbols had to be drawn in the squares to substitute for letter combinations or sounds. In one puzzle, for example, the composer used the cent sign (¢) for the letters CENT.

Mr. Weng tried to reshape the Sunday subsidiary puzzles. He eliminated the occasional cryptic puzzle that Mrs. Farrar published, and he tried to do away with the diagramless puzzles that appeared once a month, but an avalanche of letters (twelve, he says, is an avalanche) forced him to reconsider. To add spice to the Sunday Puzzle Page, Mr. Weng accepted puzzles featuring made up "should-be words." (Sample definition: "Main boxing events." The answer, LIMINARIES, makes sense when you realize that *preliminaries* come before the main bouts.) He also permitted April Fool's Day pranks in which the horizontal answers were to be written right-to-left, and puzzles that were entirely normal except that the solvers were told not to bother entering any vowels in the diagram—no room had been left for them anyway.

Mr. Weng liberalized the format of the humorous puzzle, introducing a rectangular shape called "Puns and Twists." The 17 x 13 diagram allows the composer more flexibility than does the 15 x 15 "Puns and Anagrams" shape. One definition was "Sleat or drizzel or hurrycane." The answer was BAD SPELL OF WEATHER.

Since his retirement from the *Times* in 1977 Mr. Weng has remained active in puzzling. Several of his own new constructions have appeared in *New York Magazine*. He edits puzzle books for Times Books, and watches over the collections of reprints of puzzles that appeared during his editorship.

EUGENE T. MALESKA

Dr. Maleska became the *Times* Puzzle Editor when Will Weng retired. Dr. Maleska was born in New Jersey and was graduated from Montclair State College. He was an English and Latin teacher, and later an Assistant Superintendent of Schools in New York City. He is the first, and perhaps the only, person to have a New York City school (I.S. 174 in the Bronx) named for him while he was still alive.

Dr. Maleska's second career, crossword puzzling, spans 35 years. He is one of the pioneers of the humorous puzzle, and he invented several very successful puzzle forms revolving around the use of quotations. Four of his inventions, Stepquotes, Boxquotes, Slidequotes, and Circles-in-the-Square, are described in our glossary. Mrs. Farrar recalls that Dr. Maleska's first Stepquote puzzle received a favorable reaction from *Times* solvers, and the paper reprinted the solution two weeks after it originally appeared, with a heavy line drawn through the diagram to highlight the innovative theme.

As editor at the *Times*, Dr. Maleska has reintroduced the cryptic puzzle and has continued the other humorous puzzle forms. In addition to working for the *Times*, he edits collections of puzzles for Simon and Schuster, focusing on puzzles that incorporate quotations in some fashion. He is also Mrs. Farrar's co-editor for the long-running series mentioned above.

Being one of the old hands at cryptic and humorous puzzles, Dr. Maleska has firm theories about the nature of cryptic clues. He will take pains to analyze and improve on the constructor's work if he feels that there is underlying merit.

ELIZABETH KINGSLEY

Mrs. Kingsley, like Mr. Weng and Dr. Maleska, had two careers. A Wellesley College graduate, Mrs. Kingsley taught English at Girls High School in Brooklyn for many years. When she first encountered crossword puzzles, in 1926, her reaction was "It's fun, but what's the good?" As we have noted, her disapproval of reading habits among undergraduates at Wellesley in the early 1930s caused her to seek out a new form of puzzle. Always adept at anagrams and other scrambled-word games, Mrs. Kingsley constructed the first acrostic puzzle, which she called a Double-Crostic, at the age of 61! In six months she had made 100 of these puzzles.

A friend suggested that the *Saturday Review of Literature* would make an appropriate outlet. The magazine agreed. Mrs. Kingsley constructed puzzles for *Saturday Review* at the rate of one a week from 1934 until her retirement in 1952. She also found time to compose and publish collections of Double-Crostics for Simon and Schuster, and to carry on a lively correspondence with fans. Her correspondence eventually formed the basis for a column in *Saturday Review* called "The Acrostics Club."

Mrs. Kingsley was constantly looking for new words, especially ones that disposed of H's (that always seemed to crop up far too often), J's, and Q's. Helpful fans continually supplied her with potentially useful words.

The current Double-Crostic constructor for *Saturday Review*, Thomas H. Middleton, has continued the series of books for Simon and Schuster. He has allowed some forms of experimentation including, for example, the use of cryptic clues rather than straight definitions, and "Telestich" puzzles, which are like ordinary acrostic puzzles except that the last letters of the words constitute the spelling exercise.

EDWARD POWYS MATHERS

Edward Powys Mathers was born in Forest Hill, England, and educated at Trinity College, Oxford. He was a successful literary critic, and was well known as a poet. When he first encountered crossword puzzles he was unimpressed by the tame definitions. He set about developing a cryptic style of clue that required more of the solver than mere general knowledge. By 1926, his puzzles were featured regularly in the London *Observer*. The initial reaction to his clues was that solving required too many hours, but his style caught on, and in a few years he was under pressure to extend himself, and his fans, further.

Mr. Mathers took up the *nom de puzzle* Torquemada. This choice was excruciatingly apt, for Tomás de Torquemada was the first and most infamous Grand Inquisitor of the Spanish Inquisition. Torquemada compiled some 670 puzzles for the *Observer*, the solving of which constituted weekly ordeals.

Torquemada's method of creating a puzzle was to select a theme, frequently a bit of verse or some other quotation, and then to generate a list of pertinent words. While he pondered clues, his wife had the mundane chore of fitting the words into a diagram which she devised.

Two crossword puzzle variations invented by Torquemada remain popular in England. The first, called the *bar crossword*, involves the diagram. In place of black squares, heavy bars between squares mark the ends of the words. In a well-constructed bar crossword, just as in a conventional or cryptic crossword, the pattern is symmetrical. (Figure 4-3 is an example.)

The second puzzle variation dispenses with clues altogether. Instead of clues, a narrative with some omitted words confronts the solver. The solver is told where in the diagram the missing words belong, and the words must be deduced from the context.

Derrick Macnutt and Jonathan Crowther, successors to Mr. Mathers at the *Observer,* took up the names Ximines and Azed respectively. Ximines immediately followed Torquemada as Grand Inquisitor. Azed, a nice span of the alphabet (Z being called "zed" in England) is a reversal of Deza, referring to Don Diego de Deza, who was Grand Inquisitor from 1498 to 1507.

British crossword puzzle composers regularly use pseudonyms. Among the well-known ones are Apex, meaning "to copy, or ape, X, that is, Ximines" and Virgilius, the name of an 8th-century Irish monk with a penchant for composing acrostics. In the early days of puzzling in America, fanciful pen names such as Gregorian, Persephone, and Neophyte were seen frequently, but the use of such names has gone out of fashion. A current puzzle constructor, Mel Taub, has been accused of using a pen name, which he does not. What a coincidence, however, that the name most often seen in recent years above the "Puns and Anagrams" puzzle in the *New York Times* is an anagram of the word "mutable"! Mr. Taub insists that he had not noticed the rearrangement before it was pointed out to him.

LEWIS CARROLL

Charles L. Dodgson, better known as Lewis Carroll, composed puzzles in many forms, including short quizzes in which the answers formed an acrostic. He also wrote acrostic verses for friends and neighbors.

Carroll also invented a form of puzzle he called "Doublets," in which two words of the same length are presented to the solver, whose task is to get from one word to the other by an intermediate chain of words. The magazine *Vanity Fair* ran a competition from March 29 to July 26, 1879. Each week's issue contained three Doublets; the competition was to find the shortest chain. The shortest Doublet in the entire competition, clued "CARESS PARENT," needed only two links, CAREST and PAREST. The longest Doublet, "Put ROUGE on CHEEK," required 16 links. You may enjoy working out this one for yourself. Doublets remain popular today. They are published under several names, including "Ladder-grams" and "Word Ladders."

II
SOLVING

Galileo observed, "you cannot teach a man anything; you can only help him to find it within himself." And so, the "discovery procedures" presented in this book are strategies to help you think of words you can't recall immediately, and to help you arrive at words that are not in your everyday working vocabulary.

Not all educators believe that all people can learn a rational approach to thinking. Nonetheless, experiments have demonstrated that people do improve their ability to solve problems by adopting a disciplined strategy.

You may say: "Solving crossword puzzles is no big deal. Either I can think of the right word or I can't." You are probably correct in large measure. However, there are certain principles that you apply, perhaps subconsciously, when you solve a puzzle. We believe that increased awareness of these techniques on your part will accomplish two things:

1. It will make you a better solver.
2. It will start you thinking along lines that will prove helpful when you start composing puzzles.

3
Solving Conventional Crossword Puzzles

How long a time lies in one little word.
—Shakespeare, *King Richard II*

By "conventional crossword puzzles" we mean the familiar puzzles printed in your daily newspaper. These puzzles differ from cryptic puzzles (the ones printed in British newspapers, for instance) in two respects:

1. Definitions in conventional crossword puzzles are more or less straightforward, with only occasional wordplay. Definitions (which we call "clues" to stress the distinction) in cryptic crossword puzzles challenge the solver in diverse ways, not limited to a simple "dictionary" definition.
2. The answers in conventional crossword puzzles interlock completely. That is, every letter is part of a word reading "Across" and a word reading "Down." Cryptic crossword puzzles, in contrast, have unchecked letters, letters appearing in only one word, either "Across" or "Down."[1]

GETTING STARTED

Where to Begin?

To anyone about to tackle a puzzle of sufficient difficulty to present a challenge, we recommend these methods for finding a starting point:

---

[1]Will Rogers once remarked that the best thing crossword puzzles ever did was to teach the general public the difference between "Horizontal" and "Vertical," the original designations for "Across" and "Down."

1. Glance over the definitions, looking for one that involves a phrase with a missing word; such definitions use underscores or long dashes to represent the word that completes the phrase, as, "Hollywood and —." These *fill-in-the-blank* definitions are usually giveaways. When you spot one you can complete, write the answer (VINE, in our example) in the diagram.
2. Start at the definitions for 1 Across. Read each definition in order, quickly, and look at the place in the diagram where the corresponding answer is to be written. The first time you think of an answer of the right number of letters, stop and write that answer in the diagram. The surer you are, the more heavily you write.

You should not have to spend a great deal of time finding a place to start. If you can't find one quickly, you should suspect that you may not finish this particular puzzle.

Now What?

Once you have found a starting point you should work systematically. In particular, you should not enter answers scattered all over the diagram, but you should try to use answers you already have as bases for other answers. It is easier to think of a "good word" when you know one or more of the letters in that word.

Testing a Hypothesis

Every answer you write in the diagram is, in some sense, a guess or hypothesis that subsequent answers will test and either verify or call into question. There are two ways of testing.

The obvious test involves filling in one or more of the intersecting answers. The more intersecting words you can fill in, the surer you can be that your original guess was correct. If you are unable to complete any of the crossing answers, your first try may have been wrong and you may have to come up with another one.

A related test involves partially completed words. Suppose that the letter at the point of intersection is an "S," and it is the last letter of the crossing word, as in Figure 3-1 at 3 Down. Is it reasonable from the definition to suppose that the crossing word is a plural or a verb in the third person singular?

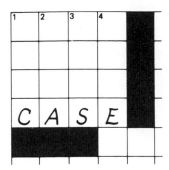

Figure 3-1   Verifying one word by reasoning about a crossing word.

You can make similar guesses and draw conclusions for the letters "ING" at the end of a participle or gerund, and for "D" at the end of a verb in the past tense. You should use partially completed words to question newly proposed answers. Some letter combinations are improbable in English: "MK," for example, or "Q" not followed by "U."

Applying these tests will help your solving efforts a great deal.

Running the Gamut

A most effective way of recalling a word you already know, given a few letters in a diagram, is to "plug in" each letter of the alphabet in turn into one of the gaps and attempt to pronounce the result, to see if the combination suggests anything useful. Often this type of alphabet scan triggers the memory. (But be sure you pronounce the combination correctly. AISLES rhymes with LISLES, but MISLED is not even close. And, of course, the combination OUGH requires careful analysis.)

When you run through the alphabet in this fashion, you naturally rule out some combinations that you "know" cannot be part of the language. However, you may fall into a trap because you "know" too much. Consider the definition "Endeavor with extravagance," and the partial word S_L_____. Suppose you decide to scan the alphabet for inspiration. SAL_____ leads to SALLIED, which might do if "endeavor" were "endeavored." You reject SBL_____ without stopping to think about it. SCL_____ leads only to words like "sclerosis" that have nothing to do with the definition. None of the other plausible combinations, SEL_____, SIL_____, SOL_____, SUL_____, or SYL_____ evokes anything useful, and you're stymied. In fact, you have fallen into a trap. You have unconsciously adopted a false hypothesis: the missing letter is a vowel. To deal fully with the situation, you must look at the crossing word. Suppose that your dilemma involves the word at 15 Across in Figure 3-2, and that 7 Down is as shown. The rules of English demand that the third letter of 7 Down be a consonant. You must reject your false notion and double check the alphabet to find SPL____, which could lead to many fine words, one of which is the required answer, SPLURGE.

Figure 3-2   Using information about one word to direct thinking about another word.

Rejecting a Hypothesis

The most difficult thing to do when solving a crossword puzzle is to put irrevocably out of your mind a word that is of the right length but is definitely wrong because it provides no help with crossing answers or it leads to implausible intersections. Be resolute: if you think a word is wrong, don't keep recalling it and trying to make it fit. You will only waste your time and frustrate yourself.

USING ALL THE INFORMATION

Subtleties in Definitions

Definitions have come a long way over the years. Composers have developed ways of giving you information, yet concealing it from you in some way. With practice you can learn to recognize the disguises.

Definition by Model. If a definition contains an abbreviated word, chances are the answer is an abbreviation, especially if it is a short word. Given the definition "Spring mo.," in which the word "month" is shortened to "mo.," you should favor APR or APL (for April) over MAY. Similarly, the definition "NCO" (for "Noncommissioned Officer") usually leads to SGT (Sergeant) or CPL (Corporal).

Another form of definition by model incorporates a speech pattern, Cockney dialect, for instance. Your task is to imagine the same speech pattern applied to the answer. The answer for "'ave a bite" may be HEAT.

Definition by Class. A definition by class consists of a word or two representing a category of things, such as "Tree." Your task as solver is to think of an item in that category, say OAK or MAPLE.

Definition by Example. This type of definition is similar to definition by class except that the roles are reversed. In other words, the definition "Oak or Maple" should lead you to TREE. "Joan of Arc" is a definition by example for SAINT.

Implied Fill-in-the-Blank. Ordinary fill-in-the-blank definitions like "Little ____Annie" are usually giveaways. Puzzle composers often try to conceal such common phrases. For instance, instead of handing you the phrase "Little ____ Annie," the puzzle composer may write "Annie, for one," or even just "Annie," in a difficult puzzle. "Sort of pone" is another way of writing "____pone," for which the answer is CORN. If the composer is indulging in a bit of wordplay, "Type of ship" may turn out to be FRIEND.

Another form of the same disguise involves two seemingly unrelated words separated by the word "or," as in "Bag or cuff." This is the same as "____bag or ____cuff," which is not a well-formed definition since it shows two missing words. (The answer is HAND.) If the conjunction is "and" instead of "or," the answer is plural.

When the sought word follows the presented word, the definition ordinarily reads something like "Corn chaser, for one." If you mentally substitute "Corn____," you'll come up with PONE.

Yet another form of the same disguise involves two words that ordinarily go together with the word "and" between them, as in "cap and gown." The constructor may define CAP as "Gown's partner." When you spot a definition like this one, you must try both possibilities, "____ and gown" and "gown and ____."

Proper names lend themselves to this disguise because so many names can stand alone as words. "Wood" can define the actress PEGGY. "Carpenter" can define the pop singer KAREN. Be on your toes.

Ambiguous Words. A clever constructor will take advantage of ambiguous words in definitions. "Put" can be present or past tense. "Close" can mean SHUT or NEAR. "Craft" can indicate one ship or a whole fleet.

Combinations. Definitions can contain several disguises in combination. Consider "Jeanne d'Arc, *et al*." The name is French, not English, which could indicate use of definition by model. The phrase "*et al*." implies that definition by example was used. Furthermore, "*et al.*," being itself an abbreviation, implies that the answer is an abbreviation. If you put all of this data together, you'll conclude that the definition really is "the abbreviation for the French word meaning 'female saints.'" The answer is STES.

What's in a Name?

The puzzles published in the *New York Times* Sunday Magazine, in some newsstand magazines and in the collections published by Times Books and by Simon and Schuster have titles. Unless the title is something like "WORDS, WORDS, WORDS," it provides some additional information for you. In "NATIONAL LEAGUE," for instance, all the thematic answers included the names of countries. A puzzle called "WIRE SERVICE" dealt with electricity.

IMPASSES

Hopscotch

Sometimes you reach a point where, because of a cluster of long words or some obscure crossings, you can't seem to continue building on your growing set of letters. If that should be the case, you need to find another starting place. The ideal place to look is alongside of, or very near to, the area of the diagram that has stumped you. Existing letters frequently suggest that certain letters of nearby words are vowels or consonants. Often the addition of one more word is an icebreaker.

Of course, you may choose to find any other starting place and begin over again. Eventually the separate sections of answers will approach one another and merge.

Halftime

Another perfectly acceptable way to deal with an apparent impasse is to take a break. Do something else for a while (but preferably not another puzzle, or any other intellectual activity), then return. A break is frequently the perfect way to refresh your ability to concentrate.

Look It Up

Some people think it isn't enough for puzzles to amuse, they must also educate. If you can't come up with a good word because you don't understand the definition, or if you need to find an obscure geographical name, educate yourself through the use of a reference book. After all, how do you think the constructor did it? Of course, if you overdo the use of dictionaries and atlases you can take some of the pride out of solving puzzles, but we see nothing objectionable in occasional consultation. Just don't get in the habit of looking up the answers in the back of the book.

When a definition has you stumped, the most obvious way to use the dictionary is to look up the definition. That gives you the best chance to remember a word that just won't come to mind. Don't skim through the dictionary looking for words that " just might fill the bill." And, anyway, you *can't* find a word meaning "absquatulate" by thumbing through Webster's for all possible three-letter words that begin HI-. If you look up "absquatulate," though, you'll (be amused to) learn that it means "to move off hastily; to depart quickly and secretively," to HIE. You'll also learn that the word has a bogus Latin etymology along the lines of "go off and squat someplace else." (It doesn't come up often in ordinary conversation, but, what the heck...)

Use of an atlas can be both educational and entertaining. While you peruse a map to find that "Austrian river," you learn a little about the geography of Austria, and your mind may wander, however briefly, to thoughts of Alps, Viennese waltzes, and ornate architecture.

Crossword puzzle dictionaries are also useful. They contain lists of definitions with possible answers. You might find five Austrian rivers to choose from, arranged in alphabetic order or in order according to the number of letters, or both. If your primary concern is to finish the puzzle, a crossword puzzle dictionary is by far the easiest way to find obscure words.

Trivia

As you solve more and more puzzles, you will gradually acquire a store of *puzzle words,* words that exist, so it seems, for the sole purpose of allowing crossword puzzle constructors to finish. After a while, such words might as well be part of your everyday vocabulary because you recall them so automatically.

There Must Be a Catch to It!

Sometimes you have to reject a possible answer because the diagram simply won't accomodate it properly: there are too few or too many squares. When this happens and you're stuck on a long, apparently thematic, answer, you may have encountered a puzzle with a gimmick (particularly if you're working on a puzzle in the *Times* or in a collection from one of the publishers mentioned above). There are two gimmicks in common use today:

1. *Substitutions.* Wherever possible, one word in the "natural" answer has been replaced by another word. The switched words have some connection. In a puzzle titled "MALEFACTORS," masculine nouns were substituted for feminine ones—producing phrases like MISTER O'LEARY'S BULL. In "INFLATION," the thematic answers involved numbers. True to the title, the numbers were inflated, as in SIX AND ELEVEN CENT STORE.
2. *Rebuses.* Wherever possible, a word or group of letters in the "natural" answer has been replaced by a shape or drawing. In a puzzle called "WINNING A GOLD ONE," the letters STAR were to be squeezed into a single square and represented by a drawn star, even in phrases like NO *CH IN MY COLLAR PLEASE. One of the funniest puzzles of this type involved answers like SECURITY BLANKET. The solver had to represent BLANK by leaving one empty square in the diagram!

Once you suspect that you are dealing with a puzzle with a gimmick, you have to gather your wits. The composer of the puzzle is trying to rattle you. Think about the title of the puzzle: what relationship might it have to the gimmick? What about the timing of the puzzle? The *Times* commemorates many events and holidays throughout the year with apt thematic puzzles. Do your hypothetical answers seem proper for some occasion or national holiday? Is there some part of the answer that lends itself to a rebus or substitution? A title like "BY THE NUMBERS" should suffice to 4WARN you.

A good gimmicky puzzle contains short answers as well as long ones using the trick, so keep alert, and enjoy yourself. Crossword puzzles that feature a gimmick are lots of fun.

The Ultimate Impasse

If you're down to the last couple of empty squares and you have exhausted all the guidelines in this chapter (and yourself in the process), you can take the extreme step taken by someone we know to finish the puzzle: decide which letters would look *pretty* in the empty squares. Under no circumstances refer to the definitions again. Write in your choices, put down your pencil, and say, "another job well done."

GAMES EXPERTS PLAY

No discussion of the process and techniques for solving crossword puzzles would be complete without some mention of the restrictions experts place on themselves. (Actually, an expert puzzle-solver is merely anyone who is working on too easy a puzzle.)

1. Use pen, not pencil. There's no room for error. You can impress people around you with this stunt. (We have heard of two ways of cheating, believe it or not. One person simply writes random letters in the diagram and is careful to crumple and discard the puzzle before anyone has a chance to look closely. Another person buys the evening edition of the paper, spends hours at home solving the puzzle, then buys *another copy of the paper* the next morning and swiftly writes in the answers for the benefit of the amazed kibitzers.)

2. Work only from the Down definitions. If you can't complete the whole puzzle in this fashion, try to guess the Across answers from the letters in the diagram. If you have to, use the Across definitions to verify your guesses.

3. Write in only the E's in the answers. In this way you can work the whole puzzle and save both energy and your pencil.

4. Don't use pencil *or* pen. Mentally work through the definitions until

you have deduced one of the thematic answers. Then say, "that's obvious," and give the puzzle to someone who still feels the need to see the answers on paper.

If these games don't challenge you sufficiently, try competition. Contests for puzzle solvers offer pressure, pleasure, prizes, and the chance to meet constructors, editors, and other solvers.

4
Solving Cryptic Crossword Puzzles

The question is ... whether you can *make words mean so many different things.*—Lewis Carroll, *Through the Looking Glass*

Many of the statements made about solving conventional crossword puzzles apply equally to solving cryptic crosswords that Americans usually characterize as "British." A solver of a cryptic puzzle should be just as aware of endings and patterns of vowels and consonants, for example, and is just as likely to benefit from guessing at single letters or particles, or from taking a break. In fact, for the solver, the essential difference between conventional puzzles and cryptic ones is just the difference between a straightforward definition and a cryptic puzzle's less direct *clue*. But that difference is great.

Our discussion of cryptic puzzles presumes that the composer is "playing fair." Leading composers and editors follow the tenets of Afrit (whose real name was A.F. Ritchie) and Ximines, who defined what constitutes fair play, or *square dealing*, and their rules, although violated by some composers, are reflected in the following explanations.

DIAGRAMS

Each *light*, the cryptic puzzle equivalent of the conventional puzzle's "word" or "answer," has at least one unchecked letter, or *unch*, a letter that is in no other light; but no light will have more than half of its letters unchecked. The diagram in Figure 4-1 is fairly typical. (Figure 4-2 contains the clues you'll use later to solve the puzzle.)

Variant diagrams also permit unches, but otherwise look quite different from the standard ones. They may have shapes like those of American diagramless puzzles, or "squares" turned 45° to be diamonds. Lights may

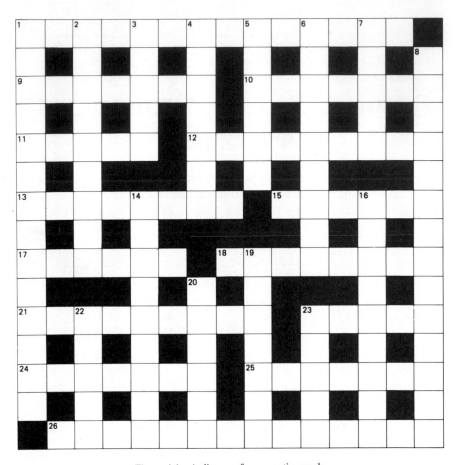

Figure 4-1 A diagram for a cryptic puzzle.

be entered in L-shaped patterns or diamonds, or as the various chessmen move, some in orthogonal or diagonal straight lines, others in squares a knight might occupy on successive moves. Some diagrams use thickened bars between white squares (and no black squares) to mark the ends of words, as shown in Figure 4-3. Variation is unlimited because no rules restrain the composer's imagination. Variety is the very spice of life for the reader-solver of the London *Observer* puzzle.

CLUES

A new solver of cryptic puzzles immediately notices two differences between definitions and clues. The first is that a clue ends with one or

Across

1. Most of the retarded group know, I hear. It's back to that bad actor, the seer. (14)
9. Back in the role of a clumsy shamus: the choosy one. (7)
10. Home with small bed by the broken gate. (7)
11. Tea makes me break out. What a waste! (5)
12. One for support on a slack net. (9)
13. A flawed facet, indeed! One's gone over to the other side. (8)
15. Meat to greet Arabs? (6)
17. French is in, but Galli-Curci isn't. (6)
18. As I heard it, a Cord is a car, Peg. Giovanni's holding one now. (8)
21. South African rants about the lava. Everyone's confused... (9)
23. ...but an inebriated African tribesman. (5)
24. Red tape reduced? Just the opposite. (7)
25. Morsels I'd bit as tough situation began. (7)
26. Short Marylanders, I, and, say, 5 natives become dancers. (14)

Down

1. Make magic before putting one finger in the state. (14)
2. You spoiled the flavor! Just two points for that one. Too bad! (9)
3. Pass a Count. (5)
4. Fifty spruce without restraint. (7)
5. In a pinch, only the Korean port will do. (6)
6. I saw the French woman in a strobe at the Star Clock. (9)
7. Egg-shaped pieces-of-eight? (5)
8. No dummies, they bring silver to quints in a rage. (14)
14. Two half-inch parts back of the helmet? No, one in front. (9)
16. The small company left the large contina business for a Southern country. (9)
19. Close the gate after D. A. leaves cathedral in a dither (7)
20. Former leader in emerging and highly populated land. (6).
22. That maple's almost enough. (5)
23. One waiting for the bemused bride. (5)

Figure 4-2   Clues for the cryptic puzzle of Figure 4-1.

more numbers in parentheses, such as "(3,7)." The numerical information in parentheses indicates the length(s) of the word(s) in the light. The clue for QUITE A SET-TO would end with (5,1,3-2), for example, with the hyphen of SET-TO being indicated by the hyphen in "3-2."

The second difference is a clue's relative wordiness. This comes about because a clue ordinarily leads the solver to the light in at least two ways. One part of the clue is a definition, as in a conventional crossword puzzle. That is, IVY might be defined by "Wall-climber" or "It climbs walls" or "Plant" or "League," for example. There may also be one or more additional definitions. "Personal enlistee (7)" contains two definitions of PRIVATE. Very short clues are apt to be double definitions. But there's usually more to a clue.

WORDPLAY

If no second definition is contained in a clue, there's wordplay instead. Several generalizations can be made about clues containing only one definition:

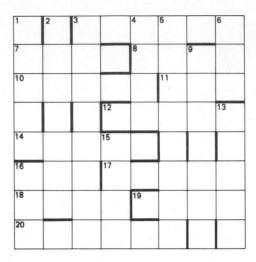

Figure 4-3   A variant diagram for cryptic puzzles.

1. Punctuation and capitalization may be used deceptively. The most natural sense of the clue as you are likely to read it may have nothing to do with the light.
2. The definition and the cryptic *hint* about the light—a pun on it or anagram of the light, for example—rarely overlap, and usually make up the entire clue or very nearly so, as in "Gift transmitted earlier (7)" for PRESENT (or PRE-SENT). If they do overlap, they usually do so completely, as in Azed's "These adorn many Scotsmen's heads (4)." The whole sentence is a fair definitional clue, but read it as "[The words':] '*These Adorn Many Scotsmen's*' heads [that is, their first letters]" and the answer TAMS, materializes.
3. There must be a *signal* as to the sort of word play that is involved. "Step off a rumpled cape (4)" contains the signal "rumpled" to indicate an anagram. Read this clue as "Step off [defines a word formed from] a rumpled [that is, rearranged] CAPE" and PACE leaps to mind.

The hint's wordplay may involve:

1. The light taken as a whole, as with PACE above
2. Its components taken naturally, such as "Stop, Stop! Ahead, ahead! (9)" to be read "[A word meaning to] stop [formed from a word

meaning] stop [with a prefix meaning] ahead [placed] ahead [of it]," namely, FORE-STALL
3. Its components taken in some unnatural grouping, such as "I say, would everybody stop! (9)" to be read "[Use a word you'd hear when] I say, 'would' [namely, 'wood,' as a definition, and follow it with a word meaning] everybody [to form a word meaning] stop," again FOREST-ALL
4. Nonconsecutive pieces of it, as in Azed's "What's tea passed around in? (5)" to be read literally, and also as "What's [a word formed from a kind of] tea [that is, CHA] passed around IN?" (CH-IN-A)

A hint that requires the solver to build up the light one piece at a time, as in 4 above, is called a *charade*. The clue "Mother and children become bricklayers (6)" leads to MASONS (MA + SONS).

Various forms of wordplay are used. We categorize them as follows:

1. Anagram—as with the clue given above for PACE.
2. Reversal—as in "The small army unit returned for a Kennedy (3)" read as "The small [that is, short or abbreviated] army unit [a *det*achment] returned [that is, is read from right to left] for [that is, to yield a word meaning] a Kennedy [that is, TED]." Were the clue to be written for a vertical light, the word "returned" might be replaced by "stood up."
3. Homophone. (sound-alike)—as in "Story's end, I hear (4)," read as "[The word defined by] story is [the same as the word meaning] end, [at least insofar as] I [can] hear." The light is TALE, a homophone for "tail."
4. Hiding—as in "Edge in the middle (3)," read as "[The word meaning] edge [can be found] in tHE Middle," HEM.
5. Homograph (spelled-alike)—the exploitation of a pair of words spelled alike, but having entirely different meanings and origins, as in "Light, wicked thing (6)," read as "[The word meaning a] light, [a] wicked [that is, having a wick] thing," CANDLE. The word "flower," for example, is frequently used to mean a body of *flow*ing water in hints of this kind. Because homographs needn't be pronounced differently, this form is indistinguishable from the simplest form of pun, for example "WASHINGTON POST (7,7)" which, because "post" means "mail," could only define CAPITAL LETTERS.

Wordplay may be compounded by having an anagram participate in a charade or camouflaged by indirection. Indirection occurs when the composer defines the word or abbreviation needed for solution instead of using it directly in the clue; for example, "army unit" defines detachment above. Proper names are used in charades as well, but are often indicated only by the use of the words "a girl," "a guy," or the like.

Abbreviations (signaled by "little" or "small") and other short forms such as Roman numerals, compass points, and articles in foreign languages, appear frequently, especially in charades. Consider, as an easy case, "Current events from all points (4)." This clue is meant to be read, "[A word meaning] current events [is formed] from [the letters identifying] all [the compass] points [that is, N, E, W, S—NEWS]." An extreme example is, "At any rate, the French will surround a wit playing with three points (9)." This can be read (tortuously) as, "[A word meaning] at any rate [is formed because] the [in] French [LE] will surround [the words] 'a wit' playing [that is, scrambled] with three [compass] points [E, S, and S]." The light is L(EASTWIS)E. Charades pose the greatest challenge, and therefore solving them will be most satisfying.

A pronoun with no antecedent may refer to the light (first or third person, I or it), the solver (second person, you), or the composer (first person). A number in a clue often refers to the light at the corresponding number in the puzzle.

COMBINING FORMS OF WORDPLAY

Charades and other types of clues often involve components that are forms of wordplay themselves:

1. Beheading and curtailing: a "beheaded prelate" is RELATE and "endless joy" is JO in this type of wordplay.
2. Heads and tails, etc.: the "head of state" is S, "last of the Sioux" is X and so is "the heart of Texas," although the latter could as easily be EXA, in this style.
3. Selection: "Most of the party" might be PRT, "some of the people" might be EOL, "dimethyl 2-6-4" is IHE (the 2nd, 6th, and 4th letters), and "a bit of trouble" is T, R, O, U, B, L, or E, when wordplay of this variety is used.

Each clue written by a square dealer obeys certain inflexible rules. The clue forms a grammatically correct (set of) phrase(s), clause(s), or sentence(s). It contains a proper definition of the whole light, correct as to part of speech, number, tense, etc. The grammar of the hint is also correct. For example, if the word "I" is to be understood as the letter "I," it is not followed by "am." "I will be," on the other hand, is grammatically sound whether "I" refers to the pronoun or to the letter.

The whole clue always makes some sort of sense, but often a sense other than the one that leads to the light. There is always a signal to the hint unless the hint is a homograph.

SOLUTION

To decipher a clue, look first for a word or group of words at the beginning or end of the clue that might be a "dictionary" definition. Then try to find a signal in the remainder to find out what type of wordplay is involved.

The words used as signals could fill a fair-sized book, but a few common ones are listed here:

1. Anagram—bad(ly), poor(ly), broken, ravished, damaged, ill, sick(ly), awkward(ly), clumsy, destroyed, wild(ly), confused, changing, new, drunken(ly), off, wrong(ly), upset, reformed.
2. Reversal—back, over, up, left, westward, rising, returns, upset, turning, North or West, contrary.
3. Homophone—hear, say, perhaps, maybe, possibly, sounds, and an exclamation point (!) or question mark (?) at the end. The question mark often signals an outrageous pun.
4. Hiding—in, contains, seen, some, part of, within, without, find, inside, outside.
5. Homograph—(no signal needed).
6. Charade—gets, for, to yield, produce, in, around, before, after, with, and, eat, about, holds, or nothing at all if no reordering of the parts is needed.

A signal like "in" is ambiguous, so be prepared to give up a line of attack that seems fruitless. If there is no signal, think in terms of multiple definitions (especially for short lights) or a homograph.

If you have trouble finding the words used in the wordplay, they may only be defined in the clue rather than provided directly. It is then time to return to what you think is the definition. Try to think of words of the proper length that fit the definition. You may find unobvious meanings for the words in the definitions, such as "that which flows, a river" for "flower," "more numb" for "number," or "one who sews" for "sewer."

Don't spend more than about half a minute with each clue the first time you try . If you are ever going to solve the puzzle, at least one or two of its clues will yield to you fairly quickly. The answers you obtain will help you discover the crossing lights. The more letters you know in a light, the longer you should persist in trying to complete that light.

The easiest lights to find are, paradoxically, those that are "hidden." This is true because you don't have to think of them, all you need to do is find them. In a clue with an appropriate signal—*e.g.*, "in"—look at sequences of consecutive letters, ignoring spaces between words. If you spot a sequence that forms a word of the correct length that is defined by the first or last few words of the clue, you have "seen the light." The light hidden in Will Shortz's clue "Insane Roman at heart (4)" is NERO.

Be particularly alert for a signal indicating an anagram. The light's length will almost always help you figure out quickly what letters are in the anagram (unless the anagram is merely part of a charade). Be particularly suspicious of numbers, proper nouns, and rare words. These often participate in anagrams. Convert the numbers to Roman numerals or to spelled-out words (SIX for 6). When you think you've assembled all of the anagram's letters, write them down somewhere or, better yet, use tiles or cubes from some word game. Look among the letters for common particles—prefixes, suffixes, or roots—and separate these, leaving the remaining letters alongside. Look among these for additional particles until you form whole words, including the right one. The *Anagram Dictionary*, devised and compiled by R. J. Edwards, might help you find longer anagrammatized lights.

Guess at long multiword answers. An embedded three-letter word may well be THE, so try it. Short initial words are often prepositions like FROM or TO or BY, so try one.

If you don't appear to be getting anywhere, work on the longest unsolved clues. The weight of many words makes it harder for the composer to misdirect you.

As you complete more of the puzzle, start doing some wild guessing based on the letters you have. The clues may be of no help, but if the light is something like _N_Q__, the answer may well be unique. Even if you can only narrow the choice to a dozen words, the list may shrink to one abruptly as you match the words against the clue.

Another fruitful avenue of attack when about half of the puzzle is solved, especially after a break, is to have another crack at the longest lights. These are the ones most susceptible to sudden inspiration. Putting particles or short words together might just work and give you quite a leg up on the rest of the puzzle.

The last resorts of a solver are the *Funk and Wagnalls Crossword Word Finder,* compiled by E. I. Schwartz and Leon Landovitz, and *Cassell's Crossword Finisher*, compiled by John Griffiths and published in England. They list words by pairs of nonconsecutive letters.

VARIANT PUZZLES

Not all cryptic puzzles have clues of the types discussed above. Some have more difficult and less standardized clues, other have clues that lead to lights in somewhat different ways.

To take two of the most common types of nonstandard puzzles:

1. Printer's deviltry—the light itself is deleted from its place of concealment as a hidden word in the clue and the remaining spaces are closed up to form new words without any rearrangement of the letters. An example is: Why does a bride have tows after a wedding? (7). EARRING (modify "tows" to read "to wEAR RINGs")— Apex, in *Games and Puzzles*, No. 41 (10/75), P. 29.

2. Misprints—a single substitution of one letter for another is made in a word in the definitional portion of each clue. An example is: The beginning of another free day (4). ARID ("day" for "dry", A ("beginning of Another") + RID (= "free")—Apex, in *Games and Puzzles*, No. 44, (1/76), P. 39.

In dealing with printer's deviltry, look for incongruous words or proper nouns to find where the clue is to be split. To cope with misprints, look near one end of each clue (that's where you find definitions) for a word spelled with fairly common letters; it is the one most likely to be transformed into another valid word by a single substitution.

The manner of entering lights into the diagram is also varied to lend spice to a composition. One or more ciphers can be used, for example, by replacing every letter in lights Across with the one following it in the alphabet, every letter in lights Down with the preceding one. Some set of related lights may be totally unclued. More than one letter may be needed for each square. One or more letters may be omitted from ("letters latent") or added to each light. These are only some of many devices composers of cryptic puzzles use.

Puzzles using devices such as these are most challenging, but detecting the device is not part of the challenge. The device is always described quite clearly in instructions accompanying the puzzle.

In these variant puzzles the term "light" refers only to the combination of letters actually entered in the diagram. The word that satisfies the clue is called an *answer,* and the process of adding or deleting letters or making other changes is called *transformation.*

CODA

A sad fact to be faced by Americans who enjoy cryptic puzzles is that most of these puzzles are composed by and for Britons and therefore use uniquely British idioms, words, place-names, spellings, and abbreviations. If you have trouble with the puzzles you encounter, it may just be because you wouldn't know a lorry's bonnet from its boot—if it had one, that is. You must either educate yourself or seek different puzzles. But, take heart, cryptic puzzles composed by and for Americans appear to be growing in popularity and you may soon be able to find them in reasonable quantity. They already appear in *The Nation, Atlantic Monthly, Harpers,* and *Games* magazines and sometimes in *The New York Times.* Try your hand at our offering—Figure 4-2 contains the set of clues and the diagram is in Figure 4-1. You should now be well-primed to try it. Figure 9-4 contains its annotated solution.

5

Solving Humorous Crossword Puzzles

A good pun may be admitted among the smaller excellencies ...
—James Boswell, *Life of Samuel Johnson*

Humorous puzzles, which are known by different names in different
publications ("Puns and Anagrams" in the *New York Times*, for instance),
have diagrams that look just like those of conventional crossword puzzles.
However, humorous puzzles are close in spirit to cryptic puzzles. Their
clues incorporate many of the devices found in cryptic crossword puzzles,
including anagrams, visual (homographic) and auditory (homophonic)
ambiguity, reversals, abbreviations, and miscellaneous signals.

In Chapter 4 we discuss methods of deciphering cryptic clues. We also
describe *square dealing*, which means that clues follow rules of grammar,
and the fact that cryptic clues almost always provide two avenues of
approach to the desired lights. Humorous puzzles frequently dispense
with square dealing and the double approach to lights, and there may be at
least this much explanation: the typical 15 x 15 cryptic puzzle has about 30
lights, compared to about 70 in a good humorous puzzle. Now, if the two
puzzles are alloted the same space in a publication, there will of necessity
be much less room available for each clue in a humorous puzzle than there
is for each one in a cryptic puzzle. The constructor of a humorous puzzle
is therefore restricted with respect to the wordiness of clues.

A Briton who is experienced at solving the puzzles in the London
Observer would, no doubt, consider our humorous puzzles trivial and
probably unfair. However, they are not inferior puzzles. Indeed, we could
argue that the compilation of a conventional crossword is more difficult
than compilation of a cryptic puzzle. We admire the skill and patience of a
constructor who can find words to fill a 4 x 7 or 5 x 6 rectangle and not

need any black squares. So far as clues go, all we can say is that they follow different rules.

In general, solving humorous puzzles is just like solving other types of crossword puzzles. Once you enter an answer into the diagram, try to use it to help find the crossing words.

Use Chapter 4 as reference, even though the clues in humorous puzzles are tame compared to cryptic clues. Here are some specific guidelines for solving the clues found in typical humorous puzzles:

1. A clue does not have to contain a dictionary definition of the light. Clues usually contain at least one word that suggests a definition, but that word may not be the appropriate part of speech. J.F. Kelly once presented the clue "For aplomb, do pies." The light was POISED, even though "aplomb" is a noun, not an adjective.

2. Humorous puzzles tend to overemphasize anagrams, and you should assume that the light you seek is an anagram of one or more words in the clue. POISED is an anagram of "do pies" in the previous clue. If two or more words in the clue make the anagram, they need not appear together in the clue. G. Buckler once gave "He goes to a resort near Reno" as the clue for TAHOE (rearranging the letters in "He ... to a").

   If the clue contains a proper name, you can be pretty sure that name is part of an anagram. Buckler once used "Tie Nell with this" for LINELET. (You see the rearrangement of "Tie Nell," of course.) You can be equally sure of an anagram when you spot initials in a clue. J. Arensberg's "What one M.D. is" led to DEMON in one puzzle.

   Look for seemingly extraneous words or abbreviations. A common method of incorporating the letters ET is to throw a gratuitious "et cetera" into the clue. The fact that the phrase is spelled out rather than abbreviated is a tipoff.

3. Numbers play two roles in clues for humorous puzzles. The first is simple substitution for their letter look-alikes, as in Dr. Maleska's clue "Zoology 101A required Ph.D." Here "101" is a substitute for "IOI." This clue reflects ideas in both the preceding guidelines. The light, OPHIDIA, is made up of the numbers/letters "101A" and "Ph. D.," which are not adjacent. OPHIDIA is the zoological suborder to which serpents belong. That might be the subject of a course called "Zoology 101A," but it is not directly defined in the clue.

As in cryptic crossword puzzles, letters may be signaled by their Roman numeral equivalents. "Five" often signals V, for instance.

The second role numbers play is to indicate which letters of a long word in the clue are to be extracted for the answer. In the clue "Direction 242 swine headed," the numerals indicate that the answer involves the second, fourth, and second letters of "swine," giving WNW.

4. Words like "tea," "ell," and "you" frequently stand for their single-letter equivalents, T, L, and U respectively. Most of the letters in the alphabet have similar representations. This substitution works both ways. Maleska's clue "Describing Dept. C" produced DEEPEST when the solver switched the "C" for "see."

5. Small lights in humorous puzzles occasionally are extracts from longer words. "Carton," "direction," and "brigade" break into smaller unrelated words. A composer could use "Rear end of a car" to clue TON, as an example. "Kind of ion" could clue DIRECT. And so on.

When the composer breaks a word at other than a natural point of syllabication the result is usually surprising and amusing. Would you realize that FRIENDS is a "Kind of hip"?

6. Clues in humorous puzzles may contain partial anagrams. In other words, the clue contains letters that do not appear in the light. This type of clue usually contains words like "from" or "lots of" as signals. In the clue "Sugars exported from Odessa," the words "exported from" signal that the solver should extract some letters from "Odessa" and perhaps rearrange them. The light is OSES.

Most of the time the containing word (here, "Odessa") bears no relation to the final light. On rare happy occasions composers achieve literal sense. "He comes from a masculine background" might clue MAN or MALE; the letters to form either word appear in sequence in "masculine." (Dmitri Borgmann coined the term "marsupial word" to describe this graphic curiosity, a word with a synonym "in its pouch.")

7. The clue may not indicate all the letters in the light. R. Lake once presented "Something new in pens" for SWINE. The clue does not indicate the letters IS.

8. "Fill-in-the-blank" clues are rare in humorous puzzles because they are difficult to compose. These clues always involve puns as opposed to anagrams. The best approach to deciphering one of these clues is to read it aloud several times, listening for what could be a

common phrase in disguise. In most cases, these clues follow the cryptic precepts regarding square dealing; a parenthetical phrase frequently provides help in the form of a secondary definition. In the clue "Justin ——(careful chap)," repetition of "Justin ——" suggests two possibilities—TIME and CASE. The word "careful" leads to CASE.

These guidelines may make clues in humorous puzzles seem easy, and many are. The answers in good humorous puzzles are longer than those in typical conventional puzzles, more than compensating for some easy clues, though, and so these puzzles are about as hard to solve as any other variety.

Try them. You'll like them.

6

Solving Diagramless Puzzles

Choice word and measured phrase—Wordsworth

Solving a diagramless puzzle is not nearly as hard as it may seem. You really have very much the same task you have with a conventional puzzle. If you need to be convinced of this, take an *easy* conventional puzzle and cover or discard its diagram *after a brief glance*. Then solve the puzzle on another sheet of paper upon which you have drawn a square grid of the correct size. This should serve to get your feet wet. Don't worry if even this gives you some trouble. Remember, you're new at it, and diagramless puzzles usually have more helpful definitions and fewer obscure words than conventional puzzles.

HOW TO BEGIN

When you encounter a diagramless puzzle, you see all of its definitions, correctly numbered, and its dimensions. Although you have no black squares and no numbers in the grid, in a sense, all you are really missing is the lengths of the answers. If you had these you could soon complete the diagram. But you do know the length of 1 Across—its length is always one less than the number of the second answer Across! This is so, as you can verify in any conventional crossword, because each of the letters in the first word Across must be the first letter in an answer Down. If you followed (or anticipated) that little bit of reasoning, you're well on your way to becoming a devoted fan of puzzles of this most interesting type.

You've probably guessed that attempts to solve diagramless puzzles must begin with the first few definitions Across. You have the information you need to deal with these.

Consider the second answer Across. Is the number of its definition the same as the number of the definition of an answer Down? If not, the second answer must begin directly under the first letter of the first answer Across. (See Figure 6-1.)

ACROSS	DOWN
1. ...	1. ...
5. ...	2. ...
6. ...	3. ...
	4. ...
	6. or higher

Figure 6-1   Starting a diagramless puzzle.

Now let's assume the opposite is true, that the first letter of the second answer Across is also the first letter of an answer Down. Assume that the second definition Across is "4. Sea creatures" and the third is numbered "7." The basic alternative configurations are shown in Figures 6-2 and 6-3. If fewer than three of the letters in the second answer Across had started answers down, that is, if the next answer across had been numbered "5" or "6," one of the configurations in Figure 6-2 would necessarily be correct because no answer, whether it starts a new column or not, may have fewer than three letters.

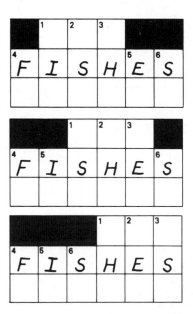

Figure 6-2   Placing a diagramless puzzle's second word Across under the first, which is three letters shorter.

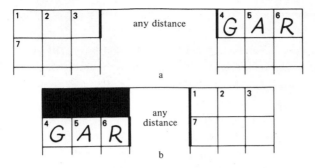

Figure 6-3 Two columns at the top of a diagramless puzzle.

If the second answer starts a new column, that column is either to the right of and on the same row as the first answer (Figure 6-3a) or to the left of it and on the next lower row (Figure 6-3b). The same sort of reasoning holds for the remainder of the puzzle.

AN EXAMPLE

Let's look at a realistic example to see if everything is clear. Try to start the puzzle for which we give the first few definitions in Figure 6-4. If you do not get all the answers before getting frustrated, look at the solution in Figure 6-6 and then read the accompanying explanation. If the puzzle presents no problem, you may wish to skip the explanation.

The first answer must have three letters because the second definition Across is numbered "4." Before or after looking at the definitions of the first three answers Down, you probably decide the answer is AFT. Four Across might start a new column and be three letters long or it might have

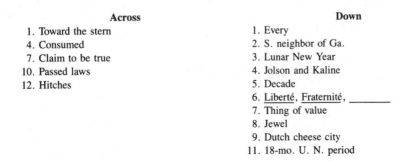

Across	Down
1. Toward the stern	1. Every
4. Consumed	2. S. neighbor of Ga.
7. Claim to be true	3. Lunar New Year
10. Passed laws	4. Jolson and Kaline
12. Hitches	5. Decade
	6. Liberté, Fraternité, _____
	7. Thing of value
	8. Jewel
	9. Dutch cheese city
	11. 18-mo. U. N. period

Figure 6-4   The first few definitions for a sample diagramless puzzle.

six letters, of which three (excluding the first) must be directly under AFT.

In either case, 7 Across must either start a new column or fall below AFT, offset to the left at least one square (because there is a 7 Down). At this point, if you have two L's below AFT or suspect that the first letters of 7, 8, and 9 Down might be A, G, and E respectively, you are likely to think of ALLEGE. That takes care of 7 Across and, with some answers Down, might even give you a fair picture of the puzzle's third row.

Ten Across poses a new problem. Let's assume your grid looks like the one in Figure 6-5. Ten Across seems likely to be four letters long (because there's no 10 Down, but there are definitions for 11 Down and 12 Across), but its definition suggests a longer answer. If you have enough information to connect your two columns with LEGISLATED, you are ready to start solving diagramless puzzles immediately. If not, you might want to study our example further and make sure you understand it all, then you will be ready. Figure 6-6 contains the solution to the puzzle fragment of Figure 6-4.

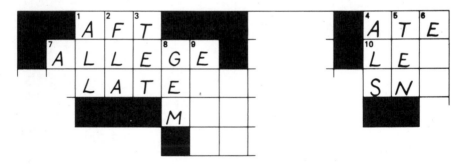

Figure 6-5   Partial solution for the sample diagramless puzzle.

Persistence is most important in solving a diagramless puzzle. If you have a few correct answers placed vertically, they may help you find a correct answer several rows down, even though the intervening definitions Across have stumped you. That one answer may tell you that some of the words above are either shorter or longer than you thought they'd be or it may help you find other vertical answers. In either case, your persistence in the face of several consecutive impenetrable definitions Across will have been rewarded.

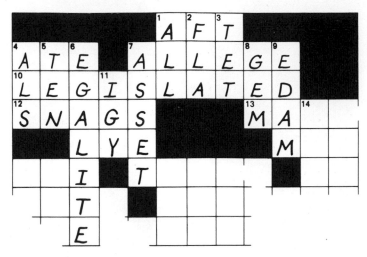

Figure 6-6 Completed solution of the puzzle fragment of Figure 6-4.

CONSIDER SYMMETRY

By the time you've completed almost half the puzzle, you should be able to tell whether or not the puzzle has any symmetry. If right-left symmetry (mirror images about the central column) has not appeared and no thematic picture has appeared, conventional symmetry is highly likely. That is, as in conventional puzzles, the puzzle's pattern of black and white squares looks the same if it is turned upside down. This information, together with the puzzle's stated size, should let you complete the diagram immediately in most cases (by turning the top half's diagram upside-down and adding the result below what you have, as in Figure 6-7). The puzzle is then "diagramless" no longer. You can usually recognize that a puzzle has right-left symmetry well before you complete the solution. If a row has more than one answer, the first and last answers have the same number of letters. If a row has an odd number of answers, the middle answer has an odd number of letters with its middle letter in the puzzle's central colum. Finally, an even number of words Down begin on each row, except when a word Down begins in the central column.

If you cannot solve the puzzle directly by starting at the top, consider other attacks. Since most diagramless puzzles have conventional symmetry, starting at the bottom is likely to be almost as easy as starting at the top, and easier definitions may make this approach even more fruitful.

Figure 6-7   The bottom of the puzzle started in Figure 6-6.

Once you have fragments of the solution at both top and bottom, you can switch back and forth as answers in each fragment give you the lengths of symmetrically opposite words in the other fragment. (Note, for example, that in a puzzle with conventional symmetry, the fourth answer Across, say, is just as long as the fourth from last answer Across.) The bottom of the puzzle shown in Figure 6-6 must look like the diagram of Figure 6-7. We have assumed that the last word has the number 61.

Conventional symmetry also permits an attack at the "waist." If the puzzle has an odd number of definitions for answers Across, the one in the middle defines the answer whose central letter occupies the puzzle's center square. If it has an even number of definitions, the two definitions in the middle define answers that surround the (black) central square(s) in the central row. You may be able to work up or down from the central row.

GRIDS

Magazines provide blank square grids for their diagramless puzzles. These are helpful, but you can obviously make your own easily. What you must keep in mind, however, is that any first guess as to the horizontal placement of the first answer Across in the puzzle is likely to be wrong. This is also true of any subsequent answer Across if three or more of its letters are the first letters of answers Down. Remember that this happens whenever two successive answers Across have numbers differing by three or more; those intervening numbers are used for answers Down. To allow for error, you should not place this answer in the grid provided. In fact, you will probably want to use a grid larger than the puzzle you are solving.

To avoid a lot of annoying erasing, you should work with a grid far wider than the finished puzzle is to be. Place the first answer in the center of the top row, and each succeeding answer Across that seems to start a new column (that is, it is immediately under no previous answer at any point) far to one side (perhaps first to the right, then one row below and to the left, of the previous answer Across, as in Figure 6-3) until its actual placement becomes certain through connection with the rest of your growing solution. The extreme placement insures that even if you have to erase the new column, you will be able to transcribe it most easily to its proper place a few characters at a time. Most solvers place small numbers in the grid that they use for solving, but some find that the numbers only get in their way due to the small size of the grid's squares.

Especially when you have made a decent start on a puzzle but have run into trouble, use your knowledge of the puzzle's dimensions. A 19 x 21 diagramless puzzle, for example, has 19 columns or is 19 squares across, and 21 rows (that is, it has 21 squares in each column). Knowing how wide the puzzle is can help you place new columns or even prove that there can't be any more. The puzzle's length helps you find its waist. Both help you connect the puzzle's halves after you've had to start working from the bottom.

ALL ABOARD

You are now ready to embark on a new and more satisfying trip into the world of puzzle-solving. Diagramless puzzles will never again intimidate you. *Bon voyage!*

7
Solving Acrostic Puzzles

The Times *and* Saturday Review
Beguiled the leisure of the crew.
———Gilbert, *The Bab Ballads*

Acrostic puzzles may appear quite formidable when you first try them. There doesn't seem to be enough information for you. The puzzle consists of a diagram like a crossword's, with numbered empty squares and a lot of black squares, and about 24 definitions followed by strings of dashes and numbers—and on first reading you know only two or three words that might satisfy the definitions. The instructions indicate, somewhat tersely, that when you solve the puzzle you will be able to read a quotation in the diagram (the black squares representing the spaces between the words), and that you will be able to read the author's name and the title of the source of the quotation (or some other phrase) in an acrostic formed by the words opposite the definitions.

To solve an acrostic puzzle you need most of the same tools you use when working a crossword puzzle—an average working vocabulary, the ability to guess at words and word fragments, a sense of likely and unlikely letter combinations, a reference book or two, and the ability to get all there is to get from a definition.

The puzzle constructor is, as usual, trying to challenge you. Definitions in acrostic puzzles are often wordier than those in crossword puzzles. They include more literary, historical, and biographical references than those in crossword puzzles. The constructor has at his disposal all the techniques for making definitions, even, in very limited markets, the devious wordplay of cryptic clues.

GETTING STARTED

In Chapter 3, "Solving Conventional Crossword Puzzles," we recommend finding one starting place and building on it. That technique doesn't

work with acrostic puzzles; the letters don't make words reading
vertically in the diagram. Get started by simply trying to think of as many
words as you can that satisfy the definitions. Write your tentative answers
above the dashes opposite the definitions, one letter per dash. Write
lightly or heavily depending on how sure you are of your guess. Figure 7-1
shows one definition and its answer.

G. Contribute   D O N A T E
                 78 9 115 182 83 40

Figure 7-1   Example of definition and answer.

If you can guess as many as three or four answers, chances are
excellent that you will finish the puzzle. If you can only guess one or two
answers, don't give up; you may still be in the running.

Let's say you are able to think of words that satisfy four definitions. As
with crossword puzzles, your answers are hypotheses, and you will test
them later. What you must do, after writing the answers over the dashes,
is to copy each letter into the square in the diagram that has in it the
number that appears under the dash. Working from Figure 7-1, you would
write D in square 78, O in square 9, and so on. Part of the diagram would
then look like Figure 7-2.

78G	79K		80A	81L	82P	83G
D						T

Figure 7-2   Part of a diagram with letters copied from an answer. (See Figure 7-1.)

In Figure 7-2, notice the small letters printed in the diagram squares.
They indicate the definition whose answer supplies the letter for that
square. (Notice, too, the letter G beside the word "Contribute" in Figure
7-1.) For now, just use these indicators to make sure you have copied each
letter into its proper square in the diagram.

After copying all of the letters in your tentative answers into their
respective squares, you will have filled in about 10 percent of the diagram.

DEDUCTION

The detective work begins now. Your objective is to reveal the quotation
hidden in the diagram. You have begun to piece it together already by
inserting a few isolated letters. (They are isolated because one satisfied
definition hardly ever supplies two letters in one word of the quotation.)

The key to solving an acrostic puzzle is remembering that the words in the diagram make sense together.

You can, and should, apply deductive reasoning to several aspects of acrostic puzzles: words by themselves, word fragments, words in combination, and total context. We describe each of these aspects below.

Words by Themselves

You should try to guess individual words whenever you have some of the letters. For instance, TH- is probably THE, although it could be THY. WA- is likely to be WAS or WAY, although WAN, WAG, WAD, and WAR are also possibilities. -RIDG- must be BRIDGE or FRIDGE, and, in any event, the last letter is E. A-D could be AND, ADD, or AID. A one-letter word is either I or A. The choice is very limited when you try to guess a two-letter word and you already have one letter. (But every once in a while a quotation pertains to TV or uses someone's initials. When this happens the best solver is temporarily thrown off. Don't worry about this challenge—you will overcome it.)

If you can guess one or more words in the quotation, even if you are not very sure, write the missing letters in their proper squares in the diagram. Hedge your bet by writing lightly so that if you later change your mind the eraser won't rub through the page. Suppose you have completed -RIDG- to form BRIDGE. (See Figure 7-3.) Your next step is to copy the letters B and E to their proper spots in the list of words opposite the definitions. The B in Figure 7-3 goes above the dash with the number "14" under it, in the word defined by definition "P." The E goes above the dash opposite definition "Q" with the number "19" beneath it.

Figure 7-3   Use of identifiers.

As you copy a letter from the diagram to a dash in one of the words, look again at the definition for that word. A single letter, even if it's not the initial letter, can bring a word to mind.

With some good guesses on your part, regarding both the original definitions and the words you guessed from a few letters, you should have completed one or two more words in the acrostic. As you did in the beginning, copy the letters from these words to their correct squares in the diagram, and look to see if the addition of these letters helps you to guess more words in the quotation.

Don't be afraid to take some wild stabs. You can go a long way on intuition when solving these puzzles, even guessing a long word from only a few letters. It is perfectly reasonable to guess that _E__E_E is BELIEVE, for instance, or that _E_P__ is PEOPLE. (Of course, many other words might be correct. The fun and pride of solving acrostic puzzles come from taking chances, trying to make as much as you can out of the least amount of information. Besides, the word PEOPLE shows up a lot more often in quotations than does, say, BEDPAN.) Even if your guess is wrong, *some* of the letters may be right because of the way letters combine in English. If BELIEVE is wrong, RELIEVE may be right. (Watch your spelling—DECEIVE is not an alternative.)

Word Fragments

In Chapter 3 we discuss the technique of surmising bits and pieces of words from context and from definition. Apply the same technique to acrostic puzzles. If a definition implies that a plural word is in order, try an S at the end of the answer. Similarly, you can infer a verb in the past tense from an equivalent form of definition. (But be careful, because many definitions that appear to lead to verbs in the past tense are in reality adjectives. "Frightened" may define AFRAID, not SCARED—an example of the composer's use of ambiguity.)

Be alert to the possibility that word fragments will emerge in the quotation as well as in the word list. The letter G at the end of a long word is probably preceded by IN. If the next to the last letter of a word is V, the last letter is likely to be E. Going one step further, you should assume that any three-letter word with one letter in the right place is the word THE. You can deduce other, longer word fragments, such as TION from T__N and ICAL from _C_L.

Lastly, don't overlook the fact that the initial letters of the word list form an acrostic. You may deduce the author's name, or you may recognize a word in the title of the source material.

Every letter you place can be a source of inspiration.

Words in Combination

Just as you can guess individual words from a few letters, so you can guess whole phrases from a few words, or even from partial words in some cases. As you gain experience and confidence in solving acrostic puzzles, you will take more and more chances, trying to build longer and longer strings of words that fit in context. Here too, a wrong guess may include some right words or letters.

There are two basic ways to deduce word combinations:

1. Sudden recognition of a common phrase. It would be impossible to list here all the short phrases you might recognize. It would also be pointless since our intent is to make you aware of the possibility without doing the work for you. In any event, here are a few combinations you should look for:

    IN THE, ON THE, TO THE, ONE OF THE
    A LONG TIME
    AS WELL AS
    IT IS

2. Analysis of grammar and context. Again, it is not practical to attempt to compile an all-inclusive list, but we have some ideas to start you off.

    a. Nouns and pronouns (used to) agree with their associated verbs. A two-letter word followed by WERE is probably WE. It can't be IT, *as it were*. In the same way, a two-letter word followed by WAS is likely to be IT or HE, not WE.

    b. Some words don't belong together. In the last example, a two-letter word followed by WAS cannot result in IN WAS or OF WAS.

    c. In ordinary English sentences, nouns precede verbs, and adjectives precede nouns. Faced with the combination in Figure 7-4, we might reason as follows: SOME should be followed by a plural noun. Put an S at the end of the long word. Copy the S to where it goes in the acrostic. Any help there? No? Back to the quotation. What comes after SOME thingS? A verb, possibly HAVE or WERE or COME, but write in an ending E anyway.

    Remember, we're describing a process of supposition here. It's entirely possible that the correct words in Figure 7-4 are SOME UNDISCIPLINED KIDS, or any of a multitude of similar constructions. When you leap to conclusions, as we have done here, you will sometimes regret your hastiness, as we have at times. So hedge your bets. Write lightly until you are sure of your guesses.

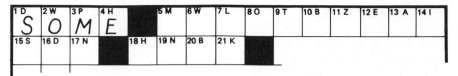

1 D	2 W	3 P	4 H		5 M	6 W	7 L	8 O	9 T	10 B	11 Z	12 E	13 A	14 I
S	O	M	E											
15 S	16 D	17 N		18 H	19 N	20 B	21 K							

Figure 7-4   Analysis of words in combination.

When you guess a phrase, follow the same procedure you use when you guess a single word. Transcribe the letters in the completed phrase to their proper locations in the acrostic, and check the definitions again to see if lightning is about to strike.

Total Context

By "total context" we mean use of three dimensions to test a hypothetical letter. In particular, the initial letters of the acrostic actually are part of three words: a word in the quotation, a word in the acrostic, and a word in the author's name or title of the source material. To a lesser degree, the second letters of the words in the acrostic also have a three-dimensioned characteristic. This means that you have three points of information to use when conjecturing tentative answers. Consider the portion of a puzzle shown in Figure 7-5a. With no other information, you can make no statement about letter 35X. It may be a consonant or a vowel. But if you also have the information in Figure 7-5b, you should conclude that 35X must be a vowel. This certainty should permit you to concentrate on, and ultimately to select one of a small number of likely answers for definition "X."

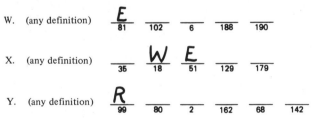

W.   (any definition) $\underset{81}{E}$ $\underset{102}{\quad}$ $\underset{6}{\quad}$ $\underset{188}{\quad}$ $\underset{190}{\quad}$

X.   (any definition) $\underset{35}{\quad}$ $\underset{18}{W}$ $\underset{51}{E}$ $\underset{129}{\quad}$ $\underset{179}{\quad}$

Y.   (any definition) $\underset{99}{R}$ $\underset{80}{\quad}$ $\underset{2}{\quad}$ $\underset{162}{\quad}$ $\underset{68}{\quad}$ $\underset{142}{\quad}$

Figure 7-5a   Total context.

	34 M	35 X	36 A
	B		L

Figure 7-5b   Total context.

OTHER THOUGHTS

The very nature of the quotations selected for use in acrostic puzzles is of value to you as solver. They are chosen for their humorous, lyrical, or evocative properties, or philosophical succinctness. We have noticed some common attributes of quotations in acrostic puzzles:

1. More often than you might expect, a word, especially a long one, is repeated within the quotation. This means that if you have two long words of equal length with some letters common, and with other letters corresponding to blanks, you should visualize the result if all the letters you have were present in both words. If the merger is plausible, both words may be the same. Suppose, for example, that your emerging quotation contains these two eight-letter words: SU__IV__ and _U_VL__R. If you mentally superimpose the two, the result is SU_VIV_R, which must be SURVIVOR. Repetition may involve word roots rather than whole words. CARELESS and CARELESSNESS may both appear, for instance.

    Less commonly, a word appearing in the quotation also appears in the title of the source material.
2. The constructor, having to deal with someone else's words, cannot inject unusual letters into the puzzle. Therefore, in a quotation of about 200 letters, you should expect the common letters (ETAOIN SHRDLU, according to one list) to be present in natural proportion. The letters W and H always seem to show up frequently due to words like WHO and HOW that appear frequently in quotations.
3. Quantifying words like SOME, MOST, NEVER, EVERY, and ALWAYS appear frequently. The words AMERICA, PEOPLE, BELIEVE, and EXPERIENCE show up out of proportion to their occurrence in everyday conversation (unless you are running for political office).
4. If a long word begins with E, the second letter may be X. This is particularly so if the second letter is also the second letter of a long word in the acrostic list.
5. Many quotations are autobiographical reminiscences. Therefore, if the first word of the entire passage is a one-letter word, it is more often I than A.
6. Assume that all one-letter words are the same.

FINAL WORDS

You will discover a tempo to the process of solving acrostic puzzles. At first the paucity of known letters allows you to make only slow progress. But with a few correct assumptions and some lucky wild guesses the pace quickens. At some point you will be absolutely certain that you can finish the puzzle. You work frantically, trying to write in several letters at the same time, each addition triggering the answer to a previously unsolved definition, each new letter added to the diagram inspiring the brain to produce still more phrases out of the remaining unfilled letters. Finally comes the denouement. You put down the pencil and read for the first time the complete solution—the quotation, a list of words (only some of which you knew at all a short time ago) and, haltingly, the name of an author and the title of a book.

What fun!

III
COMPOSING

Perhaps you are starting to read this part of the book with misgivings. You feel that you could never compose a crossword puzzle. Please put your doubts aside. If you can solve puzzles, and maybe even if you try but cannot finish them, you can compose them. All you need is a little instruction and some resoluteness of purpose. You may not sell your first puzzle; it is most unlikely that anyone has ever done so. But the first sale will swell your heart with pride when it comes, and it will soon be followed by many others. And will it be followed by riches? No, hardly that. Fame? In a *very* small circle, perhaps. But satisfaction will certainly come from knowing that millions of people want what you can produce for them.

Even before you sell puzzles, you can create them as gifts for the solvers among your friends and relatives. What gift could better express your love and consideration than your own creation, a personalized puzzle? (See Chapter 13 on Marketing for a reference to a business venture based on this idea.)

The chapters that follow treat the same types of puzzles mentioned in Part II. Again conventional puzzles, those likely to be most familiar to you, are at the top of the list. These may be the easiest to compose, but once you've got the knack, you will want

to move on to other forms. Now, it's time to begin. Here is a list
of the equipment you'll need.

1. Basic writing tools: pencil with hard lead, a block eraser, good writing surface, and good lighting.
2. Scratch paper. For crossword puzzles, we recommend pads of graph paper ruled into ¼-inch squares. You can fit four 15 x 15 grids, or two 15 x 15's plus one 23 x 23, or six 13 x 13 grids on a single side. One pad lasts a long time, and you don't have to draw lots of lines. For acrostic puzzles, any scratch paper will do.
3. A good dictionary. (But beware, the dictionary is meant to help you verify spellings or "hoped-for" words. It is not meant to be a source of cabalistical reconditeness—obscurity.)
4. Other reference books (optional): Special crossword puzzle dictionary, foreign language dictionaries, gazetteers, concordances, and/or encyclopedias.

8
Composing Conventional Crossword Puzzles

Proper words in proper places—Jonathan Swift

Most conventional crossword puzzles conform to a few simple rules:

1. The diagram is square, with an odd number of squares in every row and column.
2. Every answer is at least three letters long.
3. The pattern of black and white squares looks the same if the page is turned upside down. (Mathematically, this means that the pattern is symmetric about its central point.)

This chapter tells you how to compose conventional crossword puzzles. It contains:

1. Observations about a sample puzzle.
2. Exercises for an orderly initiation into the mysteries of composition.
3. Explanation of some rules you will have to obey in composing marketable puzzles.
4. A step-by-step analysis of the composition of a sample puzzle.
5. A discussion of more sophisticated techniques used in composing puzzles of higher quality.

THE BASICS

Figure 8-1 contains a diagram for a relatively simple composition. The puzzle has no theme, no answer more than seven letters long, few of the rare letters (i.e., Q, Z, X, J, K, W, V, F) and many of the common ones

Figure 8-1   A simple composition.

(I, E, S, R, A, T, L, D). The puzzle may therefore lack appeal to the connoisseur, but it serves our purposes well because it provides extreme examples of the characteristics of crosswords that are easy to solve and not too difficult to compose, namely:

1. Its rightmost column and bottom row contain no vowel other than E. In fact, only one word in the puzzle (ALI) ends with a vowel other than E.
2. Only 11 different letters appear in the 25 nonblack squares of the top (first) row and leftmost (first) column.
3. Many answers have alternating vowels and consonants. Only two

answers, both plurals, contain three consecutive consonants. Many diagonals contain only strings of vowels or strings of consonants.

What can these observations teach you about composing simple puzzles? First, avoid placing vowels other than E where they must end answers. Second, there are only a few letters that are good to use to begin answers. Third, avoid words with strings of consecutive vowels or consonants. (Note, however, that an S at either end of a word, next to another consonant, is more likely to help you than to hinder you.) These are the first lessons and very valuable ones.

You've probably noticed that some words occur much more often in crossword puzzles than they do in conversation or in a novel. This is true because the answers in a puzzle must interlock completely. Every letter of every answer in the top row and leftmost column of a puzzle must begin an intersecting answer. Almost half of these letters are vowels, but far fewer than half of all English words begin with vowels. This phenomenon is typical of those that make certain words valuable to composers: words that begin with vowels, words that have few vowels (for use in the top row and leftmost column), and words with no vowel other than E (for use in the bottom row and rightmost column). Here are lists of four-and five-letter words in the three categories. (*Puzzle words*, those rarely seen outside of puzzles, are starred and should be avoided.)

Words that begin with vowels (in alphabetical order):

ABASE	ALAN	ARES	EKES	ERODE
ABED	ALAS	*ARIL	ELAN	EROS
ABET	ALINE	AS IS	ELATE	EROSE
ABUT	ALIT	*ATEN	*ELEMI	*ETAPE
ACAD	ALONE	*ATES	ELITE	*ETES
*ACER	ALOP	ATONE	EMIR	ETON
ACES	ALUM	ATOP	EMIT	EVEN
ADELA	*AMATI	AVON	ENATE	EVER
ADEN	ANILE	*EBON	ENEMY	EVIL
ADORE	ANODE	ECON.	ENOS	*EWER
AFAR	APACE	EDEN	EPIC	EWES
AGAR	APED	EDER	ERAS	I-BAR
AGATE	APER	EDIT	ERASE	IBIS
AGER	ARENA	EGAD	ERATO	ICON

IDOL	ODER	ORAL	OTIC	UNAN.
*ILONA	ODIN	*ORALE	OVAL	UNIT
IMAM	OKAPI	ORAN	OVATE	UNITE
IRAN	OLIVE	ORAT.	OVEN	UPON
IRATE	ON ICE	ORATE	OVER	URAL
IRENE	ONUS	*OREL	OVINE	USED
IVAN	O.P.E.C.	ORES	ULAN (BATOR)	UTES

Words most easily used at the top or the left of a puzzle (or a corner):

SASS	TARA	TOSS	TAPS	PRAT	POST
STATS	START	ROTS	SPAT	PAST	PORTS
STARS	STRAD	*SORA	SPAD	PARD	PARA
TSAR	DARTS	*TORA	PADS	SPOT	APORT
RATS	TADS	DOST	*DAPS	STOP	RAPT
TARS	DRAT	PATS	PART	POTS	ROTO
SARA	SOTS	PAST	STRAP	TOPS	PROTO-

Words most easily used at the bottom or right of a puzzle (or a corner):

ESSES	*REDE	EDER	ETES	SEER	TRESS	STEED
SERE	STERE	TEDS	ESTER	DEER	TREES	DRESS
*RETE	REDS	SEED	REED	STEER	DETER	*SEDER

These lists should help you complete the exercises that follow.

Before you try your first composition, there is an important principle you should understand. The first place you should attack a partially completed puzzle is the square where the diagram and the letters in it give you the least freedom, that is, the square that simply must contain one of only a few letters. For example (see Figure 8-2) if a square follows an initial D in a vertical answer and it is surrounded by vowels in the crossing horizontal answer, you must place an R in the square. In general, there are two things that might restrict your choice of letters for a particular square:

1. Neighboring letters and the rules of English spelling dictate that only a few letters are candidates for the square, as in the example above.
2. There are few acceptable answers that can be placed in either the horizontal or the vertical string of squares including the one in question. For example, if you need a four-letter answer of the form

O__L, to avoid obscure words, you must make the third letter an A. The second letter might be a P, R, or V.

If the square you are filling is restricted for the second reason above, but more than one answer might be used in the direction that led to your decision to attack that square, list all the answers. Then try each one in turn, starting with the ones that seem to fit best with the letters already placed in nearby squares, until you fill in an entire region of your composition satisfactorily. The tables at the end of this chapter can help you decide in what order to try the words on your list.

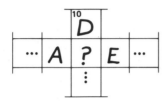

Figure 8-2   A square that must hold a particular letter, R.

First Exercise

Now apply these principles to the problem of Figure 8-3. Complete the diagram with six different ordinary three-letter English words. (We suggest you· do this and all subsequent composing exercises on separate sheets of paper. Composers use about a quarter of an inch of eraser for every two inches of lead and you don't want to erase through a page of this book.) Stop reading until you have found a solution, then read on to see how an experienced composer might solve the problem.

You can fill a puzzle's diagram most easily with words that have alternating vowels and consonants. Most three-letter words begin with consonants. Therefore, the pattern of vowels and consonants in the diagram should be the one shown in Figure 8-4.

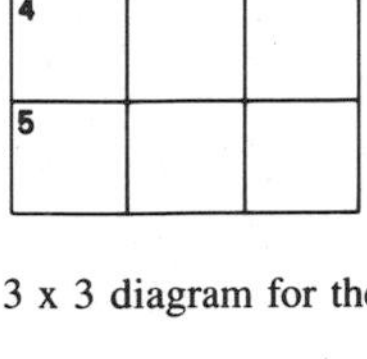

Figure 8-3   A 3 x 3 diagram for the first exercise.

Figure 8-4   Best places for vowels (v) and consonants (c) in a 3 x 3 diagram.

The vowel most often found at the ends of words is E. Let E be the last letter of 2 Down and 4 Across. The vowels that most often appear in nonfinal positions are A, O, and I. Make A the second letter of 1 Across. If the second letter of 1 Down were also A, 2 Down and 4 Across would be identical. Make that letter an O instead.

Letters which begin large numbers of three-letter words are S, T, R, and D. Let 1 Across start with an S. (See Figure 8-5.) T could start either 5 Across or 3 Down, R neither, D either. To fill the diagram with common words, use the T for 1 Across and 3 Down, the D for 1 Down and 5 Across. Three Down and 5 Across must end with the same letter. The letters which end the most three-letter words are T, N, and D. The N does nicely here. The center square could take any of several letters: R, D, W, or P. (Figure 8-6)

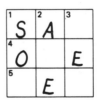

Figure 8-5   Vowels that let you complete the 3 x 3 diagram most easily.

Now move on to the significantly more difficult problem of Figure 8-7; try to complete the diagram before reading the next paragraph.

The first "key square" of the problem is the initial letter of 16 Across. Because this square precedes a final R, the rules of English spelling practically require that it contain either a vowel or the letter R. If it's an R, the next letter across must be a vowel (for similar reasons), which would mean that the word at 2 Down ends with two vowels. For the time being, ignore this possibility and proceed on the theory that 16 Across begins with a vowel. The choice of vowel can be postponed.

If 16 Across begins with a vowel, the next key square is the second

Figure 8-6 The simplest 3 x 3 composition.

letter of 16 Across—and it must contain a consonant. Go through the consonants alphabetically to find words that might fit at 16 Across. That is, first think (vowel)-B-(vowel)-T. You don't have to think too hard about "which" vowels. (After all, there were no written vowels in ancient Hebrew.) If you say to yourself, "uhBuhT," the words you're looking for come to mind soon enough. List all the common ones you find in alphabetical order by *second* letter: ABET, ABUT, OBIT, EDIT, ALIT, EMIT, OMIT, UNIT, and EXIT. Use these as the bases for further work in the order of their likely value in crossing words. Since more common 4-letter words end in IL than in EL or UL; more in LE, DE, NE, and ME than in BE or XE; and more in AR, ER, and OR than in UR, a reasonable, if somewhat arbitrary order is ALIT, EDIT, EMIT, OMIT, OBIT, UNIT, ABET, ABUT, EXIT. Make no list of the words for 2 Down because they are too numerous.

Try each of the words on our list above at 16 Across and next concentrate on the letter at the intersection of 3 Down and 13 Across. Continue the process as long as necessary to find a solution.

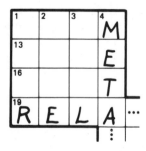

Figure 8-7 A second exercise: a typical corner.

Figure 8-8 shows solutions to the problem of Figure 8-7. The first two solutions contain only common English words. Each of the other two contains one proper name. We avoided phrases and foreign or obscure words.

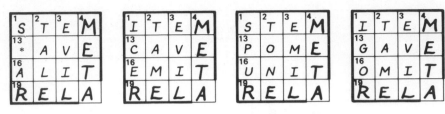

* = C, P, or E

Figure 8-8   Solutions to the second exercise.

How did you do? Don't be discouraged even if you gave up after an hour of trying. You'll improve with practice and we chose our example more for realism than for simplicity.

More Challenging Exercises

Now look at the 9 x 9 diagram of Figure 8-9. Can you think of four intersecting nine-letter answers for 4 and 5 Down and 13 and 16 Across? Try to find answers that will make it easier for you to complete the composition:

1. Answers that have alternating consonants and vowels.
2. Answers with S, T, R, P, or D in each (starred) square that will contain the first letter of a crossing word (at 5, 10, 12, 23, 25, and 27 Across and 16-21 Down).
3. Answers with E, S, R, T, D, or L in each square (marked with †) that will contain the last letter of an intersecting word (at 1, 2, 3, 6, 7, and 8 Down and 1, 9, 11, 22, 24, and 26 Across).

Some compromises are always necessary at this stage, so don't hold out for perfect answers. Our choices are shown in Figure 8-10, but they are not the only possibilities by any means.

We say that the diagram of Figures 8-9 and 8-10 has four *corners*. We use that term for any almost rectangular collection of white squares. A long answer which crosses the corner's apparent boundary is said to "bridge" corners. Each nine-letter word in this exercise bridges two corners.

Now, fill in the diagram of Figure 8-10. Follow this principle: attack next the corner which seems to you to present the greatest difficulty. The reason for doing this is the same as one that underlies the method given

* First letter of a four–letter word
† Last letter of a four–letter word

Figure 8-9   A 9 x 9 diagram.

above for choosing a particular square to attack. If the task you have cannot be completed, you will find out quickly by tackling the most difficult aspects of the task first. If you discover that you cannot complete the task, you can go back to the last letter or answer you chose as "probably but not necessarily the best" and discard it in favor of another. If you have tried all possible letters or answers in that place, you must go still further back and discard a letter or answer chosen even earlier.[1] In the present case, if you cannot complete a corner, you should discard one of the 9-letter words and replace it with another. When you run out of replacements, you should replace a different 9-letter word. When you run out of 9-letter words, you should modify the diagram, and so on.

Figure 8-11 shows one solution to the problem of Figure 8-10. The numbers at the corners of the diagram show the order in which we attacked the corners. The numbers in the lower right-hand corners of individual squares show the order in which we attacked them in completing each corner.

---

[1]A procedure such as the one described here is called "backtracking." Backtracking is a technique used intuitively in problem-solving and it is applicable to all sorts of problems, including solving crossword puzzles (and solving mazes, by the way). Yet its use is most important in a task such as composition that leans so heavily upon many interrelated assumptions. Understanding the principles of backtracking, as presented here, should give you an edge over the merely intuitive backtracker.

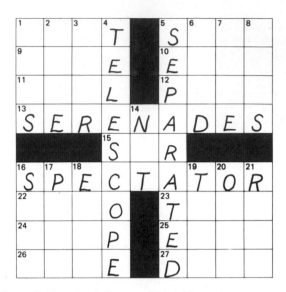

Figure 8-10   A 9 x 9 diagram with helpful nine-letter answers.

Figure 8-12 shows another solution for the problem of Figure 8-10 but one that arose from adding another condition to the problem: to use as many different letters of the alphabet as possible. To derive this more interesting solution, we first placed rare letters (X, K, Z, Y, and V) where they seemed most likely to fit and proceeded as before. ("IS UP" comes from the phrase "The jig _____.")

Now that you've had some realistic practice in the art of composing puzzles, you might try to fill in the relatively undemanding 15 x 15 diagram we used in our opening example. You should attack the starred squares first because they are the points of intersection of the diagram's longest answers. (Figure 8-13 is a blank diagram you can copy.)

As a next exercise, take simple diagrams similar to the one in Figure 8-13 and fill them in. Diagrams for easy puzzles in newspapers and in newsstand publications will do nicely. Ignore the published definitions and make up your own compositions. You can even compose while you are solving. If a corner stumps you, ignore the offending definitions and treat the corner as an exercise in composition.

Restrictions on Compositions

If you hope to market your own puzzles some day, you should be aware of some restrictions beyond those listed in the first paragraph of this chapter.

Some of these restrictions apply to diagrams, others to answers. Some are universal, others are relaxed by some editors.

A composition must be thoroughly interlocked. That is, every white square must be connected to every other white square by a chain of white squares. In addition, no region of the puzzle should be connected to the next by fewer than two answers. Otherwise, the *blind corner* that would be created would be in practical terms a separate subpuzzle, not integrated into your composition. (See Figure 8-14.) No more than about one-sixth (⅙) of a diagram's squares should be black, say 38 for a 15 x 15 puzzle (since $\frac{1}{6}(15)^2 = 225 \div 6 = 37.5$). A 15 x 15 diagram should contain no more than about 78 answers. Criteria for other sizes vary, but a fair guideline is that the average length of an answer (number of white squares divided by half the number of answers) shouldn't fall below 4.8. For sizes commonly used, this guideline comes close to criteria established by some editors, namely:

Size	Editors' Word Limit	4.8 Guideline[2]	Number of Black Squares
15 x 15	78	78	38
17 x 17	100	100	48
19 x 19	124	125	60
21 x 21	142	153	74
23 x 23	172	183	88

Note that larger puzzles should present greater challenges, so the fact that they contain longer words should not be surprising. Some editors adhere rigidly to the limit on black squares. Others relax this rule often, especially for puzzles of great appeal.

Answers must be in good taste and found in some respectable reference work—a dictionary, atlas, encyclopedia, or the like. No two answers should contain any form of the same root word unless they carry out the puzzle's theme as a result. For example, use both ROCKY and ROCKING only if ROCK is the theme of your puzzle. Many types of answers are acceptable only in limited quantities. These are listed below in order of increasing acceptability.

---

[2] 25/72 times the square of the number of letters per row.

Figure 8-11   A completed 9 x 9 diagram with indications of how the composer developed the puzzle.

Figure 8-12   A more elegant composition based on the diagram of Figure 8-10.

1. Foreign words having no English cognates (related words) or usage;
2. Foreign words having English cognates;
3. Plurals of family names;
4. Variant spellings, dialectic words, obsolete words;

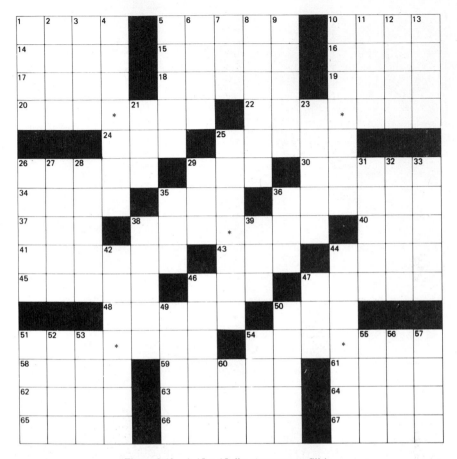

Figure 8-13   A 15 x 15 diagram you can fill in.

5. Uncommon words having a prefix of RE- meaning "again";
6. First names *not* those of well-known persons;
7. Combining forms;
8. Abbreviations;
9. Puzzle words;
10. Parts of phrases (multiple words);
11. Plurals formed with a final S.

Answers of the forms listed above should account for no more than 10% of a puzzle's answers altogether. No two answers of types 1 and 4 should ever intersect because this leaves one square most solvers will not be able to fill.

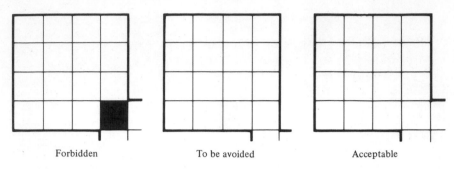

| Forbidden | To be avoided | Acceptable |

Figure 8-14   How a corner connects with the rest of a diagram.

An Example

The next sections of this chapter describe the composition of a typical thematic puzzle, one with several related answers or definitions to interest the solver. We follow the composer's reasoning as the puzzle moves from inspiration to completion. The basic steps along the way are:

1. Selection of a theme;
2. Listing of candidates for thematic answers;
3. Formation of a skeleton composed of thematic answers;
4. Provisional placement of black squares;
5. Development of a first valid solution;
6. Improvement of the solution;
7. Composition of definitions.

Note that your first compositions will probably lack themes. A theme places constraints on a puzzle and makes its composition more difficult. Yet, that is precisely why we have chosen a thematic puzzle as our example—because the theme poses problems whose solutions are interesting and instructional.

The Theme

One day we were thinking about the names of American cities and were struck by the fact that many of them are foreign phrases or names. It occurred to us that we might build a puzzle around the names and define them as phrases. For example, "Red stick: French" would define BATON ROUGE.

We began with a list of suitable names, ordering the list by the lengths of the names:

Name	*Length*
BATON ROUGE	10 or 5 + 5 (That is, could be two five-letter answers)
LOS ANGELES	10 or 3 + 7
SAINT LOUIS	10 or 5 + 5
SAN ANTONIO	10 or 3 + 7
DES MOINES	9 or 3 + 6
LAS CRUCES	9 or 3 + 6
PALO ALTO	8 or 4 + 4

We could fit more of these into a single puzzle if we had the answers cross one another, so we looked for pairs of entries (as in Figure 8-15) that could

Figure 8-15   One way to place thematic answers in a 15 x 15 diagram.

intersect without violating the rules governing a crossword's symmetry. (We tell how we went about finding them later in this chapter.) Several

Figure 8-16   Skeleton with short thematic answers added symmetrically.

possibilities appeared. Some of these, in the form of skeletal diagrams, or *skeletons*, are shown in Figures 8-15 through 8-18.

We chose to proceed from the last of these skeletons because it seemed to present the fewest and least difficult problems. In this diagram, as opposed to the others:

1. Thematic answers were not bunched too closely.
2. They fell in the rows and columns where they bridged corners most conveniently, that is, those rows and columns three to five squares from the diagram's borders.
3. They led to no requirements for masses of black squares.
4. They left the most troublesome letters (C, G, and two U's in this case) in places where we could use them fairly easily.

Figure 8-17 Another possible skeleton.

(Tables at the end of this chapter help you make such decisions. Don't worry about these details at this point.)

Provisional Placement of Black Squares

We next proceeded to place black squares where they seemed most likely to simplify our remaining tasks. We started by marking off the corners of our puzzle with *fingers*, slender strings of black squares protruding from the diagram's borders. We placed them, as Figure 8-19 shows, in such a way as to equalize the areas of the corners (because large corners are difficult to complete) and to leave the letters M and N at the ends of answers and G and U at the beginnings of answers, because we can use

Figure 8-18   A skeleton with six long thematic answers.

these letters easily in these positions. The next black squares to be placed were those nearest to the thematic answers. These gave us answers of reasonable size, fairly convenient starting and ending letters elsewhere (initial O, D, R, and O at 26 Down,[3] 35 Across and 53 and 54 Down; final O, S, R, and N symmetrically opposite). The four remaining black squares were placed to leave us with a word count of 78 and no nonthematic answer having more than seven letters. We now had our allotted 38 black squares.

---

[3]You will not want to put any numbers in your working diagram when you've reached this point. They come last. The numbers in Figure 8-19 are there so that we can make reference to them.

First Valid Solution

We next set about composing a first valid solution, tackling the most difficult problems first. The starred square of Figure 8-19 (the first letter of 49 Across) clearly deserved our first consideration because so few five-letter words end in U. BANTU, CORFU, and PERDU came to mind for 34 Down and the last had the fewest troublesome letters, so in it went. Forty-nine Across now began with D and ended with M. We couldn't think of anything better than DATUM. That gave us a start on the 5 x 5 corner in the lower righthand side of the diagram. We then placed some very common and seemingly convenient letters where other sections of the puzzle met (S's as first letters for 46 and 48 Down, S or T and L or N (because of GRAIL and GRAIN) as last letters for 10 and 18 Down respectively), and tackled each corner in turn, the largest and most troublesome ones first:

Corner	Approximate Size	Biggest Problem
bottom right	5 × 5	consecutive IO
top left	5 × 5	4 Down's last letter
bottom middle	4 × 5	44 Down, 54 Down's 2nd letter
top middle	4 × 5	5 Down
top right	4 × 5	final I of 11 Down
bottom left	4 × 5	48 Down
middle right	4 × 3	SM of DES MOINES
middle left	4 × 3	30 Across
center	3 × 3	linking up corners

Each corner's most difficult problem is listed in the table above. Each puzzle and each corner has its own personality, but it's worth noting that the most difficult problems confronting the composer tend to be (in order):

1. The longest nonthematic words;
2. The remaining bridges between corners;
3. Largest corners or sections;
4. Clusters of consecutive consonants or vowels;
5. Rare letters;
6. Less rare letters in unfortunate positions;
7. The center;
8. Remaining isolated corners.

Fingers added

Squares nearest thematic answers

Last squares placed

Figure 8-19   Black squares placed provisionally in the diagram of Figure 8-18.

Take the same approach in solving each problem: first choose letters, then whole words that place letters where you can use them easily. If a single square links sections, place an S in it. If a vowel is needed near the centers of two words, try an A. If a letter must end two words, use an S or an E. The surplus of common letters can probably be eliminated later. Don't let such a consideration delay discovery of a first valid solution.

Figure 8-20   The emerging "first valid solution" after about 2 hours.

After you have attacked the first few problems, whether successfully or not, it is again time to take stock. Are your goals attainable? Should black squares be added, moved, or deleted to increase or decrease word count? Should the form of a thematic answer be changed, for example, from KEEP IT UP to KEPT IT UP? Should two nonintersecting thematic answers be interchanged? Should you have used a larger diagram? Should you have stuck to solving puzzles? The answer to the last question, you should know, is always "No." If you have got this far you can succeed, and successful composing will satisfy you far more than successful solving ever has.

Before reading further, you might now try to find a solution of your own for the diagram shown in Figure 8-19. Our own version progressed

Figure 8-21   A first valid solution.

through the stage shown in Figure 8-20 to the form shown in Figure 8-21. Note the many flaws commonly found in such first solutions.

1. Too many common letters (inserted to make our first solution easy to find).
2. Too many abbreviations (SPR, UPO, PST, STA, AAA), rare words (ELEMI, RETE, SERE), foreign words (TES, ARS), variant spellings (IRAK), particles (-OIDS, ECTO-), etc.
3. Too many phrases (jump through A HOOP, just A LINK in the chain, to skip A BEAT, I LOVE a parade, AS TO, A STILL small voice).
4. A plural of a family name (DALI'S).

Figure 8-22   A polished composition.

Still, the solution suggests that an acceptable composition is only hours away. All we have to do now is improve the solution, step by step, starting with the most unsatisfactory corners and answers.

Polishing the Composition

Our finished composition is shown in Figure 8-22. In polishing the composition we found it necessary to insert *cheaters*, black squares that have no effect on word count, in the upper left and lower right corners of the diagram. Here are some guidelines, illustrated by references to the puzzle of our example, for moving from a first valid solution to a final composition:

1. A common shortcoming of first solutions is an abundance of words ending in S. Where two such words meet at the last letter, you can often find a plausible change. For example, change SPINS and LADS to SPINY and LADY. In Figure 8-21, 69 Across WEDS can be changed to WERE without difficulty, as in Figure 8-22. This change is good for another reason: it replaces the foreign word ARS at 64 Down with the common English word ARE.

2. Replace frequently occurring letters by rarer letters. Notice the words at 30, 38 and 43 Across in Figure 8-21. PUCE, STEVE, and TES should be changed, say to VACA ("Cabeza de _____"), OXEYE, and WES, as in Figure 8-22. The words at 35 and 41 Across, DRU and STEEP, can be changed to DIZ ("Nickname for trumpeter Gillespie") and STENO.

   To add specific rare letters to a composition, first look in a comparatively problem-free corner for a convenient square for a given rare letter, say the upper left-hand square for a Q, one row and one column in from the lower right-hand square for a Z. Then try to complete the corner with the rare letter in place. Even a sound 9 x 9 puzzle can be pangrammatic—that is, can contain every letter of the alphabet—if the composer has no other objective. See Figure 8-23, for example.

3. Eliminate abbreviations. The changes described in the previous item share this secondary virtue. Thirty Down PST ("Pacific Standard Time") is replaced by VOW, for example.

4. Replace puzzle words by ordinary words. Look at the upper right-hand corner of Figure 8-21. Six puzzle words are crammed into that small area: SERE ("Withered"), RETE ("Network"), OMER ("Hebrew measure"), ELEMI ("Varnish material"), ROTES ("Fixed routines"), and EDER ("German river"). The puzzle is definitely better after that corner has been changed completely, as in Figure 8-22.

5. Eliminate awkward phrases. Notice A BEAT at 8 Down in Figure 8-21. Revision of that portion of the composition allows the substitution of AVERT, as shown in Figure 8-22.

6. Eliminate clusters of proper nouns. The upper left-hand corner of Figure 8-21 has five proper nouns, including the variant spelling IRAK at 4 Down. One way to break up the cluster is shown in Figure 8-22. (Note, however, that we had to add the above-mentioned cheaters, and that the puzzle word AMAH has replaced

Figure 8-23   A pangrammatic (containing all letters of the alphabet) 9 x 9 composition.

IRAK. To preserve symmetry, we had to balance the first cheater by another cheater in the bottom right-hand corner of the pattern, as shown in Figure 8-22.)

7. Foreign words and variant spellings should be kept to a minimum. We have replaced several in the course of our improvements.

You may have noticed that the center of the composition changed as we moved from Figure 8-21's solution to Figure 8-22's. This is due to a "ripple effect." When we changed SANEST, at 5 Down in Figure 8-21 to VENOSE, we had to find a replacement for UNTIL at 27 Across. UPEND worked, but then the phrase I LOVE at 25 Down (which was awkward anyway) had to go. IDAHO filled in nicely, but that caused CHEERS at 44 Across to make way for CHOIRS. The point is that a single alteration may have far-reaching consequences.

Don't be dismayed by how much you have to do to improve a first valid solution. Any time you take to polish and refine a puzzle is rewarded many times over by the increased probability of sale.

You should now take a critical look at your own solution to our sample puzzle. Identify and try to correct its flaws, one by one, until you are satisfied.

Our composition still needs definitions. You can find adequate definitions easily enough, but good definitions are another matter. Turning a composer into a good composer and a puzzle into a good puzzle are the subjects of the remainder of this chapter.

THE FINER POINTS

When you are satisfied that you can turn square grids into things people can recognize as crossword puzzles, you will want to raise your sights. You will want to find interesting themes for your creations, to carry these themes through your puzzles in interesting ways, to hone your skills for placing black squares and letters, to liven your compositions with appealing nonthematic answers and definitions, and to pick up some tricks of the trade to speed up and facilitate your labors. The following material should help.

Themes

Listing the best themes for puzzles is like listing all inventions yet to be patented: it is impossible by definition. Originality, of course, is the reason. The best themes are the ones the solver has not yet encountered.

There are two dimensions to puzzle themes, subject matter and device. The key to subject matter is widespread familiarity among solvers. Literature, music, sports, dance, art, flowers and plants, animals, geography, academic subjects, minerals, history and public figures, politics, religion, the stage and screen, transportation, current events, grammar, even television, are all fit subjects. You can undoubtedly think of others.

Themes must not relate to a particularly obscure field of knowledge. Butterflies, stamps, and fencing fascinate people, but puzzles about these topics could only appear in magazines with a specialized readership. A timely theme related to a holiday or event is great if the composer can sell the puzzle at the right time. But there is little market today for puzzles on the 4-minute mile or Watergate.

A puzzle's subject is often less important to the solver's satisfaction than the device, a form of wordplay, employed with it. A device may be as simple as blind profusion—Maura Jacobson's puzzle in which over one-quarter of the definitions read "Author" brought immense pleasure to successful solvers, even those of little literary bent. The most complex devices within reason involve substitution of a symbol for a sound or combination of letters, for example, Greek letters, digits for their names (even a single symbol for both "I" and one, or "O" and zero), X for CKS, and geometric figures for their names, as in COLUMBUS ○ (circle) and TRAFALGAR □ (square). Note that the use of symbols forces the use of intersecting thematic answers. Each answer containing one of the symbols is called a *rebus*. Again, many additions to the list of devices are possible. In between the extremes are:

1. Repetition in answers (for example, STONEHENGE, REDSTONE, and LEAVE NO STONE UNTURNED).
2. Repetition in definitions (five definitions consisting solely of the word "Hudson," with answers like A BAY DISCOVERED BY CABOT and UPSTAIRS, DOWNSTAIRS MAN), also called *relocated theme*.
3. Related particles in answers (REDSTONE, WHITEFACE, and BLUE RIDGE).
4. Common puns (for winners of the Super Bowl, SCENE STEELERS and COLT-BLOODED MURDER).
5. Switches (CHARLES HORSE and CHARLENE HORSE for CHARLEY HORSE, in puzzles titled "STRICTLY FORMAL" and "WOMEN'S LIBERATION")

Themes must not be so well hidden, of course, that the successful solver does not even see them. TIRES ONESELF OUT, CAMPING GEAR, and PLUGS AWAY AT might suggest parts of a car to the composer, but the typical solver won't see how they are related unless the automotive theme is carried out elsewhere in the puzzle.

Consistency is a must in carrying out a theme. A puzzle about Super Bowl winners can use puns like SCENE STEELERS and COLT-BLOODED MURDER, but spelling either phrase correctly, sacrificing the team's nickname, would ruin the effect. If Φ appears in a puzzle using Greek letters, it may stand for either the sound or the letters PHI but not both: Φ LLIP (for Phillip) and Φ NANCE (for finance) simply would not do.

All of the puzzle's answers longer than, say, nine letters should contribute to a puzzle's theme. When shorter answers are thematic, the puzzle's symmetry should match them with one another. PALO and ALTO may appear separately in a puzzle like our sample puzzle, but each should be matched by the puzzle's symmetry with the other (as in Figure 8-16), or both with another pair of thematic entries (as with LAS CRUCES and DES MOINES in Figure 8-16 and BATON ROUGE and SAINT LOUIS in Figure 8-17).

The sum of the number of letters in the puzzle's thematic answers should be as great as possible, but at least 15% of all squares, although some editors may accept less. At least 4% of the puzzle's answers should be thematic. A reasonable way of expressing criteria editors commonly apply to thematic puzzles is shown in this table.

Puzzle Size	15% Guideline	Minimum Number of Thematic Answers
15 x 15	34	3
17 x 17	43	4
19 x 19	54	5
21 x 21	66	6
23 x 23	79	6

Remember, a puzzle's theme makes it interesting, all else merely makes it a puzzle.

Noninterlocking thematic answers, strung out across a puzzle's width, are acceptable to all editors, but solvers find interlocking thematic answers far more interesting. Interlocking answers also permit denser packing of thematic answers. Unification of the puzzle, making it a single, cohesive work of art, is another issue.

After you have selected a thematic subject and device, you should list the candidates for thematic answers. These should be at least as long as half of the puzzle's width or almost so: for example, seven letters in a 15 x 15 puzzle. Symmetry will force you in the end to select pairs of thematic answers of equal length. (The exception to this would be one or two answers going through the puzzle's center square. These must, of course, contain an odd number of letters to maintain symmetry.) You can manipulate the length of a thematic answer through the use of inflected forms and pronouns, for example, KEEP IT TO YOURSELF, KEEPS TO ONESELF, etc. Certain lengths are more convenient than others. Choose thematic answers that are, in order of preference, zero, three, five, or four letters shorter than the puzzle's width. They usually bridge corners neatly and make it easier for you to complete the puzzle. One letter less than half the puzzle's width is also a good length. Avoid thematic answers that are, in order of undesirability, two, seven, or one letter less than the puzzle's width. They often force the composer to use cheaters, which cheapen the composition.

In searching for thematic answers, first make a list of terms (or names) that pertain to the chosen subject, for example, names of composers, capitals, presidents, or flowers. You should probably do this without using a reference work. If you can't think of a term, the solver won't be able to think of one either. Look for related particles, for example, names of flowers that have names of animals embedded in them—DANDELION and SNAPDRAGON. Most often, the only relationship that will appear is enough resemblance to words in common phrases to provide grist for punning, and even that may not be obvious, so play around. Next to each term or name write words that resemble parts of it or all of it, such as STEELER vs. STEALER, and COLT vs. COLD. From there, go to expressions that contain those words, that is, the expressions such as SCENE STEALER and COLD-BLOODED MURDER that are needed to make your puns comprehensible.

Punning is only one of several devices from which you can choose. Yoking, or combining, is another. Two kings (ALAN AND RICHARD I) may appear with two princes (HAL AND CHARLES) or two Jacks (BEAU AND KENNEDY). From there, you can pursue royalty or playing cards respectively. Themes lurk in every nook and cranny of a fertile mind.

In selecting thematic answers, don't be blind to the task ahead of you. Answers with rare letters or long strings of consonants or vowels may kill your project before it is well under way. You won't see many puzzles with Steve MCQUEEN's name in them, no matter how famous he is!

Even the best of thematic subjects can conceal traps for the unwary. A subject may be quite fit, a related term totally unacceptable. You may easily recognize Pierce and Arthur as President's names, but a solver beguiled by a pun like PIERCE-D EAR may not. "Rape" may be a fine plant, but the word is simply unacceptable to some editors. A revival of interest in the Edwardian era may make Mrs. Keppel's name a household word for a time (she was Edward VII's mistress,) but it is unlikely to remain familiar long enough to make its use in a puzzle book practical. A puzzle containing one name such as Sherman Adams, Billie Sol Estes, or Bert Lance is probably unmarketable. A puzzle with all of them might be quite another matter, however. Your knowledge of some things that people, places, or objects have in common might be quite uncommon: for example, actresses who acknowledged bearing illegitimate children. One British puzzle editor has admitted failing to recognize puns on the names of former Prime Ministers (!) because the names were so common in themselves. Finally, sad experience has taught us to check our sources, especially for spelling, before investing great mental energies. A composition based on a false assumption may represent many hours of totally wasted effort.

Skeletal Composition

Once you have chosen thematic answers, several more than you expect to use so you can discard the most troublesome ones, you are ready to place them in a skeletal grid. One simple option is to string them out horizontally in widely spaced rows of the diagram. It is quite common to see a 15 x 15 puzzle with 15-letter answers on the fourth, eighth, and twelfth rows, and no other thematic entry. Such a layout gives you a lot of leeway in completing the diagram and may thus let you easily avoid obscure, foreign, or uninteresting words. This technique, however, penalizes both the composer and the solver. It removes the challenge of crossing thematic answers and limits to three the number of thematic answers.

A stack of long thematic answers next to one another is a most challenging arrangement for solver and composer alike. The placement of three thematic answers within five consecutive rows is rare indeed, but then rarity is a common criterion of worth. As with any *field of white*, a large rectangle with no black square, this layout is most interesting for the solver, but most troublesome for the composer. You should probably resort to it only if all attempts to provide intersecting thematic entries have failed.

Intersection, then, the most appealing treatment of thematic answers, is the subject of the remainder of this section on skeletal composition.

Thematic answers rarely appear one or two rows (or columns) from the top or bottom, or left or right of a puzzle. This is because thematic answers tend to be long, as noted above, and the two answers lying next to a puzzle's border tend to be equally, or very nearly equally long. This is true because perpendicular answers of fewer than three letters are prohibited. Answers of unequal length thus force the use of black squares at the end of the answer closer to the border. (See Figure 8-24.) Even if, say, two four-letter answers with a single black square between them lie along a side and a nine-letter answer lies next to them, another answer of at least nine letters must lie next to it closer to the puzzle's center to avoid two-letter answers. In Figure 8-24, for instance, the word at 17 Across must be nine letters long because 14 Across is also that length.

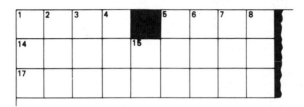

Figure 8-24 The effect of a nine-letter answer in a diagram's second row.

Further, two pairs of long answers that intersect near their centers place constraints on two large sections of a diagram and make placement of other long answers difficult.

Thus, in trying to place pairs of intersecting thematic answers, concentrate on the letters third, fourth, and fifth from each end of the answers on your list of candidates for thematic answers. These allow you to place the answers in the rows and columns where they most conveniently bridge corners.

Consider, for example, this list of American cities whose names have meanings in foreign languages (listed with longest answers first, and alphabetically within answers of the same length):

	3	4	5	5	4	3		position from nearer end of answer
BA	T	O	N	R	O	U	GE	5 + 5 = 10
LO	S	A	N	G	E	L	ES	3 + 7 = 10
SA	I	N	T	L	O	U	IS	5 + 5 = 10
SA	N	A	N	T	O	N	IO	3 + 7 = 10
DE	S	M		O	I	N	ES	3 + 5 = 9
LA	S	C		R	U	C	ES	3 + 6 = 9
PA	L	O			A	L	TO	4 + 4 = 8
	3	4	5		4	3		position from nearer end of answer

Space out the answers' letters as shown so that you can more easily find points at which two pairs of answers might intersect at symmetrically opposite points three, four, or five squares from the puzzle's borders. The ten-letter answers present the two possibilities shown above in the 15 x 15 grids in Figures 8-15 and 8-16. (In the latter, the remaining thematic answers have been placed symmetrically.) This result is fortunate. One usually needs a far longer list to achieve such results.

Have you seen how to determine whether or not the intersections you seek are possible? Let's treat the problem in concrete terms. If the same letter is the third of a nine-letter entry and the third in a ten-letter entry, as with the S's of LA*S* CRUCES and LO*S* ANGELES, then a symmetric intersection is possible if the third from last letter of another nine-letter entry matches the third from last letter of a ten-letter entry, as with the N's of DES MOI*N*ES and SAN ANTO*N*IO. (See Figure 8-17, to which we added the other ten-letter entries symmetrically as four five-letter words.)

In looking for intersections, you must focus on pairs of letters equally distant from opposite ends of answers of the same length. In the case of DESMOINES and LASCRUCES, the pairs shown by Figure 8-25 are D_S, E_E, S_C, M_U, O_R, I_C, *N_S*, E_A, and S_L. A possible intersection is found if the same pair occurs in the analysis of two other equally long answers, as with the N-S pair that is italicized above and is also the eighth to arise in considering SANANTO*N*IO and LO*S*ANGELES. This coincidence accounts for Figure 8-17.

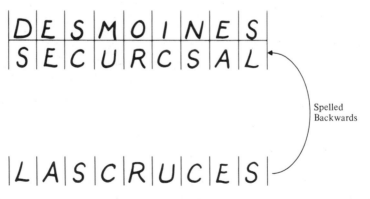

Figure 8-25   A way of finding pairs of letters equally distant from opposite ends of two equally long thematic answers.

A different way of achieving intersections is to place one long answer with an odd number of letters in the central column (or row) of the grid, to be your puzzle's *spine*. Two answers of equal length can intersect with it if they have as their nth and nth from last letters respectively, two letters that occur in the spine equidistant from its middle letter, as with:

```
                    D
                    E
              LOSANGELES
                    M
                    O
                    I
           SANANTONIO
                    E
                    S
```

That is, S, the third letter of LO*S*ANGELES and N, the third from last letter of the equally long thematic answer, SANANTO*N*IO, are equally far from the center (O) of DE*S*MOI*N*ES.

Not all thematic answers will intersect with one another. In fact, many puzzles have no such intersections at all. How then should you place nonintersecting thematic answers? They should bridge corners. (Remember, we call a rectangular section a corner, even if it isn't in a corner of the diagram.) That is, place thematic answers in about the fourth row from a border, up against or near an edge; or equidistant from two edges in a large puzzle. These positions form natural borders internal to a puzzle. Thus, each section of the puzzle along an edge has the following borders: an edge on one side; two fingers (black squares perpendicular to the edge on two sides); and a long, presumably thematic, answer on the fourth and last side. See the diagram of Figure 8-26, for example.

To determine which corners a nonthematic answer should bridge, examine its letters. Of course, some corners may already have been bridged by intersection of thematic answers. If the answer has many letters that often appear in the third, fourth, or fifth positions of words or rarely appear in those positions,[4] then place the answer accordingly:

	Common	*Rare**
third position	T L D A R I O N	H E X
fourth position	T E D S R	S H C I O
fifth position	R S E	V L A I U O

*Q, J, and Z are rare in all of these position.

Avoid a row or column that is the third from a border if the answer has letters from the set Q, J, Z, H, E, X; seek such a row or column if it has

---

[4]The judgment expressed in this and succeeding paragraphs is based on experience. It concerns not all words, only those which are easily placed in puzzles. Rare words and those with rare letters or troublesome combinations of letters do not enter into our consideration. Nor does the frequency with which words appear in ordinary writing. Therefore, our tables were not compiled by counting words in dictionaries or on pages of prose. The short tables in the text are included in more comprehensive tables at the end of this chapter.

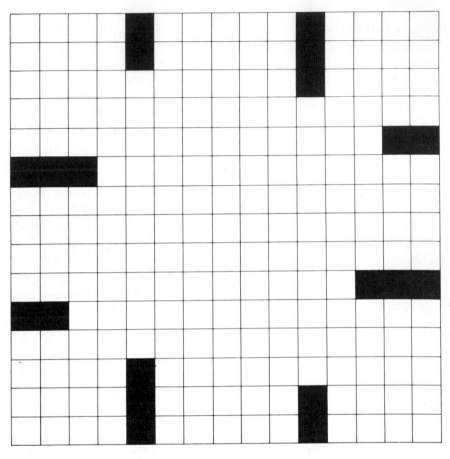

Figure 8-26   Fingers in a 15 x 15 grid, creating three corners along each edge.

many of the letters T, L, D, A, R, I, O, N. Similarly, for the ends of words, common and rare letters are:

	Common	Rare
third from end	A R D L C P V	Q Z Y F
fourth from end	R T A O I L	X U Y F
fifth from end	S T D E	X Z Y N K V O

and you should seek or avoid the rows and columns near the bottom and right of the grid accordingly.

Of course, some letters are rarer than others, irrespective of their positions in words. Letters such as Q, Z, J, and X will rarely occur in your thematic answers, so knowing where *not* to place them will be of little value. More interesting are the examples of those places where common letters are rarely found, and rare letters are most commonly found. Key facts, then, are that V is easy to incorporate third from the end of a word and O is difficult when it is fifth from the end, etc. Remember these facts when you place thematic entries. (See the tables at the end of this chapter for more data of this sort.)

When you have tentatively placed all thematic answers in the working diagram, determine its final size. This will usually be the smallest square grid with an odd number of letters on each side that contains the assembled skeleton comfortably. That is, the parallel thematic answers must not be so close to one another that you will find it difficult to complete the diagram.

Placing Black Squares

You are now ready for provisional placement of black squares. The placement of thematic answers has determined some of these already. The next black squares you place will be those that set off the corners. Most 15 x 15 puzzles have three corners per side, although many have two corners per side, especially "Puns and Anagrams" puzzles. The arrangement of three corners along one pair of opposite edges and two along the other is fine, but rarely seen. This may be due to the difficulty of finding an answer to emerge from the middle of an elongated corner as a bridge to another corner. Three corners per side may suffice for diagrams up to 19 or 21 squares to a side. Four corners per side should serve the largest common conventional puzzles, those 23 x 23. Most often the corners are bounded by fingers of three, two, or four black squares protruding from the edge between corners. (See Figure 8-26.)

The next batch of black squares, those in the rows and columns on either side of the thematic answers, are placed by reference to those answers. Some letters commonly, and easily, begin words, and some end words most frequently. Some rarely begin words, while others hardly ever end words. These letters are:

	Common	*Rare*
Start words	S T R O P F Q J G	X N Y E V
End words	S R D E T N L Y	Q J Z V I U B

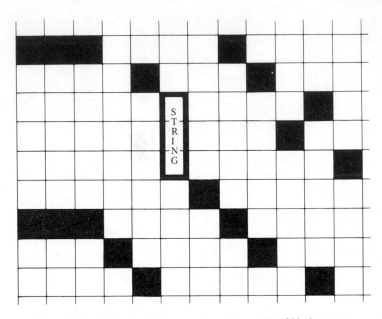

Figure 8-27   Fields of white created alongside a string of black squares.

The locations of these letters in thematic answers influence your placement of black squares. You must not forget other criteria, however. Words must have at least three letters. The puzzle must not contain so many short words as to fail to meet the editor's criteria.

A slender string of consecutive black squares within a puzzle creates a rectangular field of white on either side, with which you must be prepared to deal. (See Figure 8-27.) This is one reason that *ladders*, strings of black squares along a diagonal (see Figure 8-28), simplify a composer's task, as shown in the diagram in Figure 8-1. Another advantage applies to ladders that run from the upper right to the lower left—NE-SW, if you will (as in Figure 8-28). Here the same square is the first (or last or second . . .) of each of two different words. Since some letters, such as P, are good "first letters," and others, such as E, are good "last letters," this simplifies your task. The first and third squares of answers in NE-SW ladders are good places for rare letters, as is also shown in Figure 8-28.

Another batch of black squares appears two and three rows from the thematic answers. To place these, you should know which letters are easiest, and which most difficult to handle when they are two or three letters from the beginnings and ends of words. These are:

Figure 8-28   Ladder.

	Good	*Bad*
2 from start	A O I R T U	J Z Q K W V F
3 from start	T L D A R I O N	Q J Z X H E V
2 from end	E D R T N P L	Q J X Z F I U
3 from end	A R D L C P V	Q Z Y F

The last black squares placed are those near the center of the diagram, if these are still needed.

A few final words on provisional placement of black squares follow: Watch out for rare letters and consonantal clusters. Rare letters and strings of consecutive consonants, or vowels for that matter, in thematic answers can wreak havoc with a promising composition. At least one of the consecutive consonants, other than S (which participates in many consonantal clusters), should begin or end a word, like the last letters of 23 and 49 Across and 7, 8, and 46 Down and the first letters of 53 Across and 18 Down in the diagram of Figure 8-19. Pay special attention to rare letters and clusters and give them priority when you place black squares near them.

When black squares have been placed *provisionally*, check your word count. If your work has led to an acceptable diagram, proceed; if it has not, rework is in order.

We should comment here on how to determine a diagram's word count. You could count each answer, of course, but symmetry offers a shortcut. To find out how many horizontal answers there are, count the answers in the rows above the central row (that takes care of the top half), double that number (for the bottom half), and add the number of words in the central row. To find out how many vertical answers there are, count the words in columns in similar fashion. Count the left half, double to include the right half, add the center. Then add the two results together.

Let's look now at the example in Figure 8-19 again to see how it illustrates the points we've made. We placed the nonintersecting thematic answers in the only locations left for them and they served as bridges into the corners containing no intersecting thematic answers. These answers *could* have been placed one square closer to the puzzle's borders, but the U's near the ends of the answers favored the placements shown. We used two two-square fingers in the sixth and tenth rows and columns to establish the boundaries of corners. Remaining black squares were placed to facilitate completion of the composition by keeping to a minimum the numbers of

1. Long answers;
2. Answers ending or beginning with vowels other than E;
3. Long answers sandwiched between thematic answers or near troublesome clusters or letters.

When you have placed black squares provisionally, you may find that word count is your major problem. When this happens, consider these stratagems:

1. Removing one black square can turn four three-letter answers into two seven-letter answers that cross at their centers.
2. Adding cheaters may permit you to turn two short answers into one that isn't too long. To maintain the word count in the other direction, you will have to move the black square you deleted in a direction perpendicular to the answer you created. (See Figure 8-29)
3. Deleting cheaters may raise the quality of your puzzle. If you have black squares configured like this:

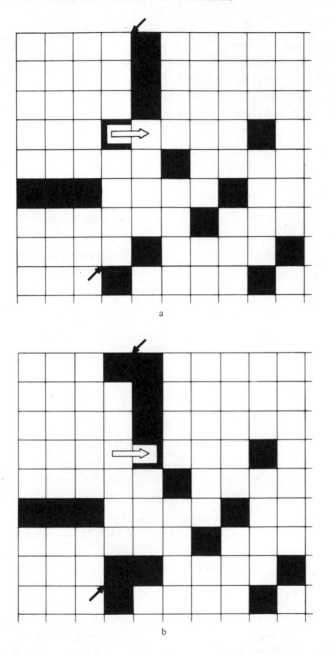

Figure 8-29   Lowering word count by adding two cheaters (solid arrows) and moving an existing black square (hollow arrow).

either square in the middle row can be deleted without altering word count, but not both.

4. Consider reducing the number of corners either horizontally or vertically especially where no thematic answer acts as a bridge. You can handle larger corners unconstrained by thematic answers. This stratagem, of course, is likely to involve a lot of reworking of the composition.

5. Don't rule out nonthematic answers that are as long as the shortest thematic ones. They can be puzzle-saving bridges, but they should be used symmetrically.

Once the black squares are in place, the tasks that remain are those that might be the *only* ones you thought about before starting this chapter: filling in letters and providing definitions. Much has been said about these tasks above, but some finer points remain to be made.

The Composition

The basic problem of simply thinking of needed answers is susceptible to a number of attacks.

1. *Funk and Wagnalls Crossword Word Finder*, compiled by E. E. Schwartz and Leon Landovitz, lists (without definitions) all words of six letters or fewer that have two specific letters in specific positions. Invest in it if you wish, but a crossword puzzle dictionary may well be all you need. It will suffice for those good old three-toed sloths, for example.

2. Keep inflected forms and common prefixes in mind. Plurals, third person singular forms, verbs in the past tense, and words beginning with RE- or IN- should be used sparingly, but they can be very valuable in difficult situations.

3. Keep an eye out for places where phrases may save the day. If you can place a preposition, article, or pronoun at the beginning or end of an answer of intermediate size, you may be able to find another word to fill out the answer and form part of an acceptable title, saying, or quotation. A few concordances (such as those for the Bible and Shakespeare) and a book of "Familiar Quotations" can help, even though "familiar" is not an editor's synonym for "acceptable."

4. For small words, complement the crossword puzzle dictionary in your library with a good atlas and lists of abbreviations.

5. For longer words, consider words in foreign languages. These must be tapped sparingly, but knowing when and how to use them can be very important. Lean to cognates, words that resemble their English equivalents, to give the monolingual solver a fair chance. Familiarize yourself with patterns that appear in various languages, for example "aa-" in Dutch, "-ich-" in German, "-oli" in Italian, "-u" in French, and inflectional endings. The *Random House Unabridged Dictionary's* concise French-, Spanish-, Italian-, and German-English sections can be valuable aids in this approach.

6. Be mindful of the patterns in which letters appear. What do all of these words and phrases have in common?

one-time	delegates
Camelot	para-medic
avocado	inoperative
ecumenical	misused
not on a bet	coverage

Answer: they all have alternating consonants and vowels, which makes them extremely useful. You can fill in relatively large fields of white, and ladders of even six- or seven-letter words quite rapidly by manipulating such words.

A final resort is trickery, using a single symbol for an alphabetic O in one word and a numeric zero in another, for example. In the extreme, IOLITTLE can be defined by "_____ Indians."

Polishing the puzzle

Use judgment when selecting words to complete the composition. There are good reasons for including and for rejecting words—if you can find alternatives.

A composition filled with uninteresting answers will bore the solver. INTEREST is an uninteresting word. No matter how clever the definition is, the solver will gain no satisfaction from thinking of INTEREST. Here are a few attributes of interesting words:

1. Lots of consonants. Words with a high percentage of consonants, though their incorporation in the composition may be difficult, keep the solver's attention.
2. High imagery. Adjectives and adverbs, which evoke images, are pleasant words to encounter. PURPLE, CRISP, SULTRY, and DOWDY are examples of evocative words.
3. Onomatopoeia and cacophony. Words like CLAMOR, SMOOTH, MOUTHY, BUZZ, and BARNACLE can almost be heard as well as seen.

Here, for contrast, are some kinds of words that, to us, are not interesting in a puzzle:

1. Ordinary words from technical and bureaucratic circles. These words are often lifeless—words like PARAMETER, HYBRID, CONSTRUCT, and INDIVIDUAL.
2. Proper names.
3. Words loaded down with prefixes and/or suffixes. The word UNRETENTIVENESS does nothing for us. Don't coin words by tacking on prefixes. REHESITATE, as Will Weng once wrote, is "a poor word."

A Subtle Refinement

You should be aware of one last subtle refinement: rewriting the entire composition so that all the horizontal words become vertical words, and *vice versa*. Modify your completed composition in any of five situations:

1. The vertical thematic answers are more interesting than the horizontal ones.
2. The theme is carried by the definitions (as opposed to the answers) and the thematic answers are all in widely separated rows. Placing them in columns may move the definitions closer to one another, catching the solver's attention.
3. The first several horizontal words are less interesting than the vertical words in the two leftmost columns.
4. The bottom row of the composition contains more E's and S's than the right-hand column.

5. In your opinion, the arrangement of black squares looks more cluttered than it does when you turn the pattern on its side.

Definitions

Prepare definitions only after the composition is complete, including all possible refinements. Depending on your personal preference, you can prepare definitions using scratch paper, or you can work at the typewriter while getting the puzzle ready for submittal.

There are several basic types of definitions, even if cryptic clues are excluded. Most common, especially in newsstand publications, is the straight "dictionary" definition. "Woody plant" is used to define TREE, for instance. Most puzzle solvers are tired of these definitions, unless their sole interest is in finishing the solution without regard for entertainment in the process. Certainly the puzzle editors don't want these definitions if they can be avoided.

The successful seller of crossword puzzles tries at every opportunity to inject variety into the definitions. This aspect of puzzling is just as important as discovery of fresh themes.

How is variety achieved? How are definitions spiced? The general requirement is that you stay away from the dictionary definition. Ironically, this means that you must use a dictionary and other reference books. A basic library includes a thesaurus, a biographical dictionary, and a gazetteer. If you rely only on your memory you will miss many good definitions, and you will miss an excellent chance to broaden your own knowledge as well as that of the people who solve your puzzles.

One valuable type of definition is *definition by example*. Using this form, you could define TREE as "Oak or elm." An advantage of definition by example is that you can choose examples in such a way as to increase the difficulty of the puzzle. "Apple or pear" is perfectly good for TREE, and would be misleading for a while, especially because POME is another possible answer. "Banyan, for instance" stretches the solver's knowledge somewhat; "Baobab" does the same, and "Acacia" and "Lebbek" get downright obscure.

You can select an unusual or secondary meaning of a word as a basis for definition. For example, TREE is also a verb, meaning "to back into a tight spot," hence, "Corner." TREE also means "to stretch shoes on a last," yielding the definition "Stretch shoes."

Treat a word as an attribute of some other word, that can be either a person or an ordinary noun. This is *definition by description*. For instance, "Kilmer's symbol of beauty" is TREE. So is "Surgeon of a sort," or "Type of frog." "Family, for one" reverses the attribution.

The last three examples are related to *fill-in-the-blank* definitions, in which the desired word is not defined per se, but is omitted from a phrase, as in "_____ of life" or "_____ of knowledge."

"Forest feature," and, less directly, "Sherwood sight," suggest TREE as a response. These associations are not so straightforward as the previous ones, and so they would make a puzzle more difficult. "Leopard's perch" is a little more direct, but compensates in that it calls up an image in the solver's mind.

Another technique, the use of proper names, is related to fill-in-the-blank definitions. TREE could be clued as "Theatrical figure Sir Herbert Beerbohm" for instance.

Literary allusions make good definitions if the references aren't too obscure. "It grew in Brooklyn" is fine for TREE.

Mild puns are acceptable in conventional crosswords. One way to introduce a pun is by writing a *definition by model*, in which a speech pattern leads to the answer by some indirect route. "Da digit afta two" is TREE.

Imagery is most important. "Picnic umbrella" evokes thoughts of pleasant outings. "Shade giver" is lifeless.

Try to use several different kinds of definitions in each puzzle.

Be careful about parts of speech. "Climbs the walls" can define GOES DAFT, but not IVY, a noun. Be precise. A definition must indeed *define* the answer. "Quest" can define SEARCH, not FLEECE or GRAIL, the object of a quest.

When you have completed all the definitions, review those that lead to words that provide access into isolated areas of the diagram. It's extremely difficult to judge this point, but you should insure that, if one portion of the diagram seems to have a lot of tough words or definitions, you modify one or more definitions to give the solver a fair shake.

One "don't" must accompany this list of "do's." Don't use any form of a word in your composition in any of the definitions, unless it's part of the theme of the puzzle.

In any event, don't panic about having to prepare definitions, do the best you can. The editor is always at liberty to make improvements. A patient editor will take the time to counsel you.

Career Planning

What types of puzzles should you now compose? We suggest that you start by composing puzzles for your own amusement. Then, compose puzzles as gifts for puzzle fans among your relatives, friends and acquaintances. What present could show more thought?

After you've reached the point where your pride and confidence in your skills are unshakable, try to sell a puzzle. Let our chapter on marketing be your guide. Start with periodicals devoted to puzzles, which buy more puzzles of all types and levels of difficulty, then move to publications with fewer opportunities. Few composers reach the top of the trade and even those who do don't become wealthy as a result, so don't give up the joys of composition because you still see a few puzzles better than any of your own.

Three Useful Tables

In the following three tables we present our opinions, based on experience, regarding placement of letters in words in crossword puzzles. You will have many occasions to disregard the information in these tables to satisfy the constraints of puzzles in progress. However, we believe that on many more occasions these tables will simplify your task by helping you eliminate problems before they arise.

Table 1 provides information to help you select rows and columns for thematic answers and place black squares near thematic answers. For example, try to avoid placing a black square so that X, N, Y, E, or V must start a word, or that Q, J, Z, V, I, U, or B must end a word.

Table 2 provides information to help you complete corners. It tells you what letters are likely to help you find crossing words. If you have a choice of letters for a square, look at Table 2 for letters that will give you the most freedom in selecting a crossing answer. For example, if you must complete the word A-ED, Table 2 will help you choose from among C, G, P, W, and X, depending on the position of that letter in the crossing word.

Table 3 can be used to finish an area where some constraining letters already exist. Consider the corner in Figure 8-30. You fill the starred square in Figure 8-30 by using Table 3 to find a letter that easily follows D near the beginning of a word, and precedes E near the end of a word. The only such letters are D (which can be dismissed here) and R.

Thematic answer:
PADDLE YOUR OWN CANOE

Figure 8-30 An example of how you might use Table 3.

Now that you know how to compose a puzzle, invest six to ten hours on a 15 x 15 crossword. You may be hooked for life.

Table 1. Positions in five- to seven-letter words where particular letters are especially easy or hard to deal with.

Position of Letters from start	
Easiest	Hardest
1. S T R D P F Q J G	X N Y E V
2. A O I R T U	J Z Q K W V F
3. T L D A R I O N	Q J Z H E X
4. T E D S R	Q J X Z S H C I O
5. R S E	Q J Z X V L A I U O

Position of Letters from end	
Easiest	Hardest
1. S R D E T N L Y	Q J Z V I U B
2. E D R T N P L	Q J X Z F I U
3. A R D L C P V	Q Z Y F
4. R T A O I L	X U Y F
5. S T D E	X Z Y N K V O

Table 2. Position in five- to seven-letter words where it is best or worst to find particular letters.

	Position from start		Position from end	
Letter	*Best*	*Worst*	*Best*	*Worst*
A	2,3	1*	3,2	1**
B	1,3	2	3	1,2
C	1	2	3	1,2
D	1,3	2	1,3	
E		1,3	1,2	
F	1	2		1,3,2
G	1	2		2,3
H	2,1	3		2
I	2,3	1	3	1
J	1	2,3		1,2,3
K	3	2	2	
L	1,2,3		3,2	
M	1,3		2	1,3
N	3	1	2,1	3
O	2,3		3	1
P	1,3	2	3,2	1
Q	1	3,2		2,1,3
R	1,2,3		1,3	
S	1	2	1	
T	1,3,2		2,1	
U	2	3		1,2
V	3	2,1	2,3	1
W	1	2		2
X	2	1	1	2
Y		1,2	1	3,2
Z		2		1

*that is, as first letter of answer
**that is, as last letter of answer

Table 3. Letters that most often precede or follow given letters in four-
and five-letter words.

Letters that often precede		Given	Letters that often follow	
Near Beginning	Near End	Letter	Near Beginning	Near End
R,L,M,B,T,H,S	E,R,L,N,M,T	A	R,L,N,M,T	S,N,L,R,T,D
A,O	A,M,R,O,U	B	A,O,E,R,U,I,L	S,E,A,O,I
S,A,I,O	I,A,O,E,U,N,R	C	O,A,H,R,L,U	H,K,E,A,T,O
A,I,O,E	E,I,A,N,O,R	D	O,E,I,A,U,R	E,S,Y,A
R,L,D,H,T,S	L,R,T,N,D	E	N,R,L,A,E	S,D,R,A,N,L,T
A,E,I,O	F,I,A,E,O,L,R	F	L,A,I,E,R	S,F,T,E,Y
A,O,I	N,A,O,I,R	G	A,R,O,L	E,S,O,A,I,H,Y
S,C,T,W,P	C,T,S,P	H	A,I,O,E,U	E,A,I,S,Y
R,L,D,H,M,T,P	R,L,A,N,T,D	I	N,L,T,R,S,D	N,L,S,E,T,D,R
E	N,A,O	J	A,O,E	A,I,O
A,I,O,S	N,R,O,A,S	K	I,E,A	E,S,Y,A
A,I,O,E,U,S,B	A,I,L,E,O	L	A,O,I,E,U	S,E,L,A,Y,T,O
A,E,O,I,U,S	A,O,U,I,E	M	A,O,I,E,U	E,S,P,A,I,Y
I,A,E,O,U,S	I,A,O,E,U,R	N	O,A,E,I,U	S,T,E,G,A,D
R,T,L,D,M,P,N	R,O,L,T,N,I,G	O	R,L,N,U,V,T,M	N,R,S,L,T,W
S,A,O,U	A,O,M,E	P	vowels,L,R	S,E,A,T,Y,H
S,A	A	Q	U	U
A,O,T,P,D,G,I	E,A,O,U,I	R	A,I,O,E,U	E,A,S,T,I,O,Y
A,U,O,I,E	E,A,T,N,I,U,O	S	vowels,T,P,L	E,T,S,H
A,S,E,I,O,U	A,S,N,O,I,R,E	T	A,O,R,E,I,H,U	S,E,Y,A,H,T
L,R,T,P,S,D	O,R,L,A	U	R,N,L,S	S,R,N,L,E
O,A,I,U,E	A,I,E	V	vowels	E,A,I,O,Y
O,A,S,T,	O,A,E	W	A,I,E,O,R,H	S,E,N,L
E,O	E,I,A,O	X	E	E,I
A	L,R,T,N,A	Y	A,O,E	S,E,L
A	A,Z	Z	A,O	E,Y,Z,A

9

Composing Cryptic Crossword Puzzles

*To ... the man who searches painfully for the perfect word ...
there is ... the constant joy of sudden discovery.*
—H. L. Mencken, *A Book of Prefaces*

Cryptic crosswords present the composer with problems quite unlike those of the conventional variety. Most significant of these is the cryptic clue. Another vital difference, less important but best discussed first, is the diagram.

While, from common origins, the American puzzle progressed to greater interconnections of words, eliminating letters with no intersection (unchecked letters or *unches*), the British puzzle exploited unchecked letters to give the composer greater freedom in completing the diagram. The cross-checking provided by total interconnection permits the American composer to use ambiguous definitions. The solver requires vocabulary skills. The composer of cryptic puzzles needs clues that lead only to a single answer, but so subtly as to retain and actually heighten challenge. The solver must be devious, employing wit rather than mere vocabulary, the needle and not the sword.

There is much to be said for this but fans of cryptic puzzles probably say too much. Subtlety is gained at the expense of challenge in the diagram's construction. In the end, solvers will forever take up the verbal cudgel for the type of puzzle they most enjoy. *De gustibus non est disputandum*.

DIAGRAMS

Many types of diagrams are used for cryptic puzzles. The type we discuss is the most common one. It is symmetric about the same point that serves

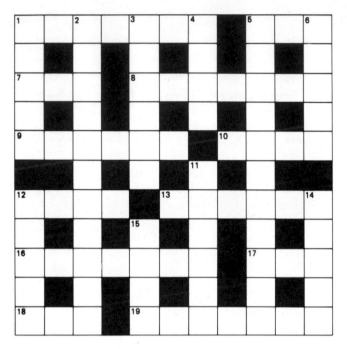

Figure 9-1   Checking at least half of each light's letters in a diagram for a cryptic puzzle.

conventional crossword puzzles, the center square. No more than one-half of the letters in any one word are unches. No word has fewer than three letters and the average word length runs close to half the puzzle's width (and length, since the diagram is square) in puzzles up to 17 x 17. A 15 x 15 puzzle might contain 24 to 32 words. Numbers are placed as they are in conventional puzzles.

In standard diagrams for cryptic puzzles, alternate letters are checked as a rule. (To find two consecutive unchecked letters is hardly uncommon, but three are never found in sequence in high-quality cryptic puzzles.) Checking of at least half of each light's letters, especially short lights, a worthy goal, is most simply achieved by the checking of alternate letters including either the first or the last letter of each light. In the case of words across, this implies that lights lie directly on the top and left borders of the puzzle at their junction, rather than one row and one column inside the borders. Symmetry, of course, then places a checked letter at the bottom right corner of the diagram as well. (See Figure 9-1.)

Blind corners, it should be clear, are every bit as undesirable in cryptic puzzles as they are in conventional puzzles. That is, it should never be possible to divide one puzzle into two by blacking out a single square.

Consecutive checked letters most often occur in cryptic puzzles in the manner shown in Figure 9-2, that is, one of two consecutive checked letters will end an intersecting light, and the other will start one. The pattern of Figure 9-3 is particularly pleasing. Because a cryptic puzzle offers the constructor a greater choice of words than conventional puzzles offer, selection of interesting words is of prime importance.

Figure 9-2   Consecutive checked letters in a cryptic puzzle.

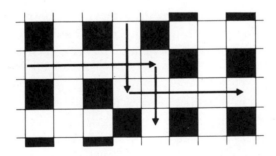

Figure 9-3   Pleasing interlock in a cryptic puzzle.

LIGHTS

Cryptic puzzles usually contain four, or, less often, two or six, lights equal in length to the width of the puzzle, or nearly so. These may be united by some theme, as in conventional puzzles, but they need not be. The puzzle's longest lights should form the basis of your composition. You should choose and place these first, preferably intersecting at the diagram's upper left (northwest) and lower right (southeast) corners.

Choose the long lights in such a way as to make it easiest for you to complete the composition. Don't choose for 1 Across or 1 Down a long light whose odd (third, fifth, seventh, etc.) letters, the ones that will be the first letters of intersecting lights, rarely begin words. Similarly, long lights that end in the extreme bottom right-hand corner must have no letters that rarely end words in odd-numbered positions, counting from their last letters. Those positions correspond to the last letters of intersecting lights.

Because the clues of cryptic puzzles involve plays on words, the lights you choose for such puzzles should be those that readily lend themselves to such antics. Such words are those that contain particles with multiple meanings like *pine*apple, dande*lion,* and re*store*; those that contain shorter and *totally unrelated* words within them, forward, backward, or scrambled, like or*dina*ry, f*amil*iar (LIMA), or pe*netr*ate (RENT); those with a fair number of common letters from which you can easily form anagrams; and others as suggested by the methods of cluing described below.

The letters at intersections of lights should generally be fairly common consonants or vowels, in positions they occupy less commonly. Why? Because these must serve as aids to solution, yet must not impede completion of the composition by the author. The knowledge that the first and last letters of a five-letter light are S and E hardly helps the solver, yet making the same letters N and W, unacceptably constrains the composer. More agreeable choices for these positions are W and D, B and R, or C and L.

As to the lights in your composition, much of what we say above about conventional puzzles applies to cryptic puzzles as well. Long intersecting lights challenge and ultimately reward the solver. Patterns of vowels and consonants play a significant role. Altogether, achieving a first valid composition is much easier for cryptic puzzles than it is for conventional puzzles, but completing it in a most interesting manner is far more important and poses many of the same problems. The *clues* make the cryptic puzzle, but the composition's lights determine to what the clues must lead. There may be no interesting way to clue UNDER.

Start filling in your composition from the upper left (northwest) corner. It is easiest to think of words in terms of their initial letters and these have been determined by the two long lights that intersect in the extreme upper left square. Use lights about as long as half the puzzle's length and width, with common consonants in the odd positions, if possible. This insures interesting and helpful crossings. Work on the upper right and lower left corners next. By the time you get to the lower right corner, difficulties will have arisen. Solve them by redoing whatever you must. Don't become so enraptured with a six-letter light that you'll hesitate to change it to complete a puzzle.

Within any particular section of the diagram, proceed as in composing conventional puzzles: solve the most difficult problems first. Then, by the time you near the end of your task and have many letters seeking a word to hold them, the letters may well be convenient ones like S-A-T- and may leave you many words from which to choose, like SPARTA, STARTS, SHANTY, etc.

Many answers acceptable in conventional puzzles are unacceptable in cryptic puzzles—those that fill-in-the-blanks or require long definitions, for example. Clues won't work with such lights.

Good sources for lights are *Cassell's Crossword Finisher* and the *Funk and Wagnalls Crossword Word Finder*, mentioned above. Of course, you must avoid the non-American entries in the former.

CLUING

A cryptic puzzle should have a set of clues about half of which are fairly evenly balanced among multiple definitions, simple charades involving anagrams, hidden lights, and charades involving no anagrams. (See Chapter 4 for descriptions of clues and their types.) These will clue the easiest lights for the solver to find and they should be sprinkled about the puzzle rather than concentrated in one area. The remaining clues may be more complex, involving charades some of whose parts are not used directly in the clue but are merely defined instead. These will be the clues the solver finds most difficult, and therefore most rewarding to solve. If the first set of clues you derive is unbalanced, look for easier clues for lights that have common letters or, conversely, harder clues for lights that have rarer letters. Don't be reluctant to change parts of the composition to get more interesting clues or a better balanced set of clues.

The quality of a clue is measured by several criteria:

1. The depth at which its true meaning is buried—deep enough to challenge, not so deep as to be unfair or lie undiscovered once the light is known to the intelligent solver.

2. Avoidance of the obscure or arcane—the clue should make no unreasonable demands on the solvers' knowledge, only reasonable demands on their wit.
3. Economy—no word should be wasted.
4. Simplicity—no more ideas should be brought to the clue than it needs.

Once you have completed the composition, you will begin to compose clues. Actually, the composition may well have grown from one or more particular words for which you already had choice clues in mind, so you need now consider only the remaining lights. First, compose clues for the lights likely to give you the most trouble, the longest lights and those with rare letters. When you get down to the most easily clued lights, you'll know what types of clues you need for balance and will have the greatest freedom to exercise your wit.

In seeking clues, look first for totally unrelated words concealed in the light or hiding at its ends. Would you find LUST in BALUSTRADE, or PETER around PERIMETER? If not, you couldn't compose clues such as: "Rail with lust in its heart and a beard badly trimmed around. (10)" or "Outside, Peter held the emir back. (9)"

Total anagrams are good things to look for next. To find these most easily and rapidly, take tiles or cubes from some word game and shuffle them around, not randomly, but by placing common prefixes (such as RE-, IN-, DE-, EX-), suffixes (such as -ER, -ED, -ES, -ING), roots (such as -ECT-, -PLAIN-, -VIS-) and common digram and trigrams (pairs and triplets of adjacent letters) such as ER, AT, EST, ENT, ANT, TLE together in groups. Of course, if you don't have tiles or cubes available, paper and pencil will do. Anyway, with a little effort, you'd probably soon spot, say, A GENTLE for ELEGANT. If so, you might come up with something like:

"Stylish, gentle, yet clumsy when one is inside. (7)" ("A" is obtained from the "one.")

Recomposition (such as FOREST ALL for FORE-STALL) and simple changes with great consequences (HIDE-OUT to HIDEOUS) are useful bases for good clues. Consider:

"Stop in the forest all at once. (9)"

"Refinished hideous den. (7)" (Replace the last letter of HIDEOUS to derive a word meaning "den.")

In looking for charades, force yourself to forget etymology and pronunciation. Otherwise, you may never realize that BEGONE = BEG + ONE or COOPERATION = COOPER + AT + ION, and you'll therefore miss:

"Plead for a leave (6)"

"Barrell-maker near ion-exchange (11)"

Once you have exhausted the basic approaches described in the preceding paragraphs, you are left with charades. Almost every letter or pair of letters lends itself to several promising treatments. Here are a few for single letters:

A—one, top grade, middleman, from French, note (in music)

B—boy's first, Ben initially, bee, note

C—see, 100, sea, about (circa), note

D—land's end, 500, Dan's first, note, dawn's first

E—end of the game, point (of compass), note, string (of a violin)

F—bad grade, loud (in music), note

G—gee, note, string

H—Cockney's Waterloo

I—one, I (first person), eye

J—jay, little John, first of January

K—Kay, quai, King

L—50, left

M—1000, measure, (of type), top of the morning, first of May

N—point, measure, little Nell, pole

O—nothing, circle, boy at heart, loop, love (tennis), egg, ring

P—soft (in music), pea

Q—queue, cue, Queen

R—are, right, King (Rex), redhead, our

S—point, pole, head of state

T—tee, tea

U—school (univ.), you

V—five, victory

W—point

X—ten, cross, kiss, heart of Texas

Y—why, end of day

Z—the end

Pairs and triplets of letters are also easy to handle, especially if you dip into abbreviations, chemicals symbols, and foreign articles, namely:

French—LA, LE, UN, UNE, LES
Spanish—LA, EL, LAS, LOS, UNO, UNA
German—DER, DIE, DAS, EIN

You must remember, however, that anagrammatizing is most pleasing to the solver when the longest words with the fewest common digrams and trigrams are involved. Thus, an anagram of the light FORESTALL that used the element STALL and, worse, defined it by the same word, "stop," that defines the whole light, is poor. The anagram LATENT for TALENT has the virtue of having a meaning neither so close as to be a giveaway nor so remote as to make cluing very difficult. But it does have the vices of a common trigram, ENT, and a common pattern of vowels and consonants. The best anagram is something like ENUMERATION for MOUNTAINEER, because the two words are long and have no linguistic root or digram in common, but have meanings sufficiently unspecialized to lead to a pleasing clue, such as "Sloppy enumeration left out climber (11)," to be read, "Sloppy [that is, anagrammatized] ENUMERATION left [as residue a word meaning] out [-of-doors] climber."

Of course, when you have found a pleasing anagram or charade, you are not done. You still need a witty clue. It is probably not possible to teach someone how to be witty. For the most part, wit depends upon vocabulary, creativity, and, most of all, practice. The only general hint apt to be of use is this one: scan all the definitions of the lights, anagrams, and parts of your charade for those which you can define in the largest number of ways. These second-level definitions may include words such as "set," "put," "let," or "note" that you can easily use in a single sentence with the desired effect. That's your clue. If the implications of our hint are unclear to you, try to see how each of the clues used as examples in this section might have been derived using the procedure described above.

If a clue involving an anagram or charade looks too easy for your intended audience, try replacing a word in that clue by another that defines it. The added level of indirection can challenge and please a competent solver. It might frustrate a novice, however, so don't add indirection capriciously. After all, it's the solvers who pay you.

An appealing device that makes a clue more challenging is this one:

Use for the dictionary definition a word or phrase whose meaning in context in the clue appears to be altogether different from the one the solver must discover. The clue, "Light, wicked thing (6)," for CANDLE has this virtue because "light" seems to mean "not heavy" rather than "a device that illuminates."

Another way to throw solvers off the track temporarily is to use a word that usually serves as a signal, in some other sense—in an anagram or charade, for instance.

Punctuation can be used deceptively where it doesn't matter, but it must be used precisely where it does matter. "Robin's-egg" is a shade of blue. A "robin's egg" is found in a nest. The "robins' egg" contains their offspring. You must say what you mean.

One last thing you must remember in devising a cryptic clue: don't leave the identity of an unchecked letter ambiguous. "Tidy up delicate lace, then add a bit of decoration (5)," read as "[A word meaning] tidy up [is formed from] delicate [that is, anagrammatized] LACE [if you] then add a bit of [that is, one letter from] DECORATION," won't do if the last letter of CLEAN or CLEAR is unchecked!

When you have a complete set of clues, polish them as follows:

1. If two adjacent clues have a related theme, rewrite them to emphasize the relationship. See 21 and 23 Across in Figure 4-2 for an example.
2. Where possible, use words with multiple meanings or words that might be signals (in place of their synonyms).
3. Unlike Naomi (that is, Ruthlessly), strip from each clue all words that are not essential to the fairness (legitimacy) of the clue or to its disguise as a normal sentence, clause, or phrase.

CONCLUSION

Like conventional puzzles, cryptic puzzles can be turned ninety degrees to interchange lights Across and Down. This should be done to a composition to gain a more pleasing juxtaposition of clues with related themes. Note, for example, the clues for 21 and 23 Across in Figure 4-2.

To gain a better appreciation of how to construct a cryptic puzzle, study Figures 9-4 and 9-5, the solution to the puzzle of Figures 4-1 and 4-2. Note particularly the four related lights of 14 letters each that frame the puzzle and the lights ending in vowels other than E. We placed these in the diagram first. The nine-letter lights were next. Finally we finished the composition from upper left to lower right, refined it with superior lights, and gave it clues.

Oh, as to cluing UNDER, how about "Beneath French-German articles"?

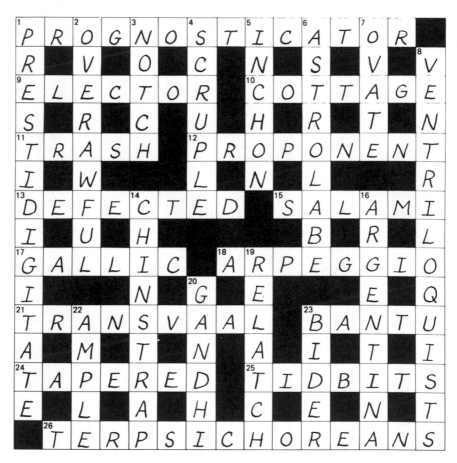

Figure 9-4   Solution of the puzzle of Figures 4-1 and 4-2.

ANNOTATED SOLUTION

^d = definition of the light or part of a charade
" " = signal as to the form of wordplay used
* = anagram (rearrangement of letters)
• = hidden word (letters in proper order with space among them)
^r = reversal (letters in reverse order)
^h = homophone (word that sounds like another)

Across

1. PROG^r (most of group^r) + NO (know^h) + STI (it's^r "back") + CATOR* ("bad" actor) = seer^d.

9. EL(ECT*)OR ("back" "in" role^r "clumsy" shamus^d (TEC*)) = choosy one^d.

10. Home^d = COT (small bed^d) + TAGE ("broken" gate*)

11. T (Tea) + RASH (break out) = waste^d.

12. One for^d = PROP (support^d) + ON + ENT ("slack" net*).

13. DE(FECT)ED ("flawed" FACET "in DEED" − A (one's "gone")) = gone over to the other side^d.

15. SALAMI (salaam) = meat^d.

17. GALLIC• ("in") = French^d.

18. ARPEGGIO• ("in") = chord^{h,d} ("heard").

21. TRANS(rants*) + VAAL (lava* "confused") = South African^d.

23. BANTU ("confused" but an*) = African tribesman^d.

24. Reduced^d = TAPERED (red tape "the opposite").

25. Morsels^d = T(IDBIT)S (I'd bit "in" *t*ough *s*ituation).

26. TERPS (Marylanders^d) + I + CHOREANS ("say" natives of 5 Down^d = Koreans) = dancers^d

Down

1. Make magic^d = PRE (before^d) ST(IDIGIT)ATE (one finger "in" state).

2. OV(E)RA(W)F(U)L (You^h "spoiled" flavor* points^d "in") = too bad^d.

3. NOTCH = (mountain) pass^d = a count^d.

4. SCRUP(L)E* (Fifty(L), spruce* "without") = restraint^d.

5. INCHON• ("in") = Korean sea port^d.

6. ASTRO(LA)BE• (the French woman^d "in" a strobe) = star clock.

7. OVATE^h (of-eight^h) = egg-shaped.

8. No dummies^d = VENTRILOQUISTS* (silver to quints* "in a rage").

14. CH (half-inch) + IN (half-inch) + STRAP^r (parts^r) = one in front of the helmet.

16. ARGENTINA• (small company (CO) "left" the large contina•) = Southern country^d.

19. Close the gate^d = RELATCH* (cathedral − DA* "leaves" "in a dither").

20. Former leader^d = GANDHI•.

22. AMPLE* (maple "almost") = enough^d.

23. One waiting^d = BIDER* ("bemused" bride).

Figure 9-5   Notes for the solution in Figure 9-4.

10
Composing Humorous Crossword Puzzles

A man who could make so vile a pun would not scruple to pick a pocket.—John Dennis, *The Gentleman's Magazine, Vol. LI*

You already know that the two elements of crossword puzzle construction are the composition itself and the set of definitions, and that you should tackle them in that order. The procedures and guidelines presented for the composition of conventional crossword puzzles generally apply to such humorous offshoots as "Puns and Anagrams" as well. But there are some special points to be considered.

Editors place heavy emphasis on long words (or low word count) in these puzzles. Themes occur only rarely. In practical terms, this means that you have to use patterns with plenty of white space, like the one in Figure 10-1, and let the words fall where they may.[1]

Minor variations on the pattern in Figure 10-1 are common, usually involving the triplets of black squares in the interior of the grid, and they do not affect the total word count of 70. Other alterations include cheaters in the corners, flanking the fingers, or in the interior. The critical feature of the pattern is that it contains only two words in the first row and two words in the leftmost column. Most crossword puzzles with three words in the top row and in the leftmost column have unacceptably high word-counts as humorous puzzles.

Composition of a crossword puzzle with only 70 words is a very challenging mental task. (All the answers, of course, must be real words or phrases—no nonsensical letter combinations pass the editor's scrutiny.) We recommend that you refer to Chapter 8 for help in composing the

---

[1] Almost all humorous puzzles use 15 x 15 patterns. We discuss only puzzles of this size.

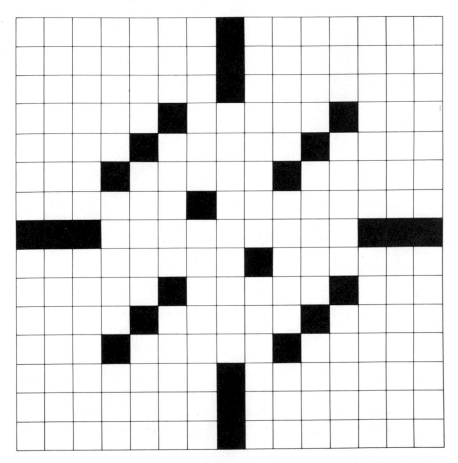

Figure 10-1 Typical humorous puzzle pattern. Darkening the center square simplifies the task of composing the puzzle, while raising the word count only from 70 to 72.

puzzle itself. The remainder of this chapter discusses techniques for making clues for humorous puzzles.

You are not bound to follow any rigid rules when writing clues for humorous puzzles. If for no reason other than space requirements in publications, puzzle editors cannot afford the luxury of verbose cryptic clues that "play fair" in all respects. Don't be afraid to be inventive. Who knows, maybe you'll discover a new kind of clue.

The guidelines that we give solvers of humorous puzzles in Chapter 5 are essentially the same ones that apply to the writing of clues:

1. Clues should, but need not, supply primary definitions for answers. If necessary, a clue can suggest a definition in a roundabout way.

2. While most editors would rather emphasize puns and other word-play, anagrams are the most abundant resources. Words in anagrams do not have to be together in the clue. Avoid the signals that make anagrams so obvious, namely, proper names, rare words, abbreviations, and numerals. A forced anagram may be the least desirable clue, and you should use one only as a last resort.

3. Some numbers have alphabetic lookalikes. You can also imply some letters by Arabic equivalents of Roman numerals.

4. Spell letters by short words: "tea," "are," "eye," and so on. You can also spell plural letters: "ease" for EE, "tease" for TT. An appealing ploy is to spell two different letters by one word in the clue: "Ellen" for LN and "any" for NE.

5. For short words: think of a long word that begins or ends with the word you're cluing and take advantage of the coincidence. (In clues of this type, disguise what you've done as best you can. "Cat tail" for NIP will nicely distract a solver who cannot reject the image of the marsh plant.)

6. Think of a longer word that happens to contain all the letters of the word you're cluing. Even if the long word has nothing to do with the short one, you can usually make something of it. You will have better luck with this kind of clue if you look for place names or proper names. You could clue ADA, for instance, as "Town in Nevada?" even though it's in Oklahoma.

7. Make a clue that is basically the inverse of the form described in the preceding suggestion. That is, find a *shorter* word among the letters of your answer. Incorporate the shorter word in the clue without regard for the leftover letters. G. Buckler once presented the clue "Candy made with cream" for CARAMEL. You should try to achieve literary sense in clues of this form, and you should use more than half the letters in the answer word in the clue.

8. You can incorporate fill-in-the-blank clues in humorous puzzles. Such clues invariably involve puns. You can get an idea by repeating aloud the word to be clued. Think of phrases that use the word. Invention of a clue like "Bronze _____ Ages (fireside topic?)" for ANDIRON ("and Iron") is very satisfying. Strive to be fair when preparing one of these clues. Supply a short parenthetical phrase that sheds light on your dark humor.

Someone once remarked, speaking of the game of chess, "when you have found a good move, look again. There's probably a better one." The same idea applies to writing clues for humorous puzzles. A clue may be mediocre, adequate, good, or outstanding. It may also not be to the taste of the puzzle editor, but that's another story.

11
Composing Diagramless Crossword Puzzles

A shapeless mass and a book of rules—R. L. Sharpe, *Stumbling Block or Stepping Stone*

No type of crossword gives the composer more satisfaction than the diagramless puzzle. This is true because the form offers so much more opportunity for creativity. The stifling square borders and constraints of symmetry are gone. The composer becomes an artist, creating a silhouette on a blank canvas.

Yet, like any art, the composition of diagramless puzzles has its discipline. Diagramless puzzles must be no larger than 23 x 23 for American markets. They should have about 82 words, unless they are 17 x 17 or smaller and destined for periodicals other than the *The New York Times*. Two-letter words remain *verboten*. Obscure words are far less welcome in diagramless puzzles than they are in conventional crosswords.

Your objectives as the composer of a diagramless puzzle are to stimulate and challenge, but not thwart, the solver. These objectives may, and should, sound familiar, but they have unique implications in the present context. The solvers of a diagramless puzzle are challenged if they cannot complete the puzzle without restarting it at a point other than the beginning. There should be answers Across, besides those in the first row, that lie under no previous answers; that is, each letter of the answer starts an answer Down. Solvers cannot place such answers in the grid definitively until they can link them with what has gone before. The more rows needed for reconnection, the greater the solver's satisfaction in accomplishing it. If the solver cannot finish the puzzle without working from the bottom up, or even, in the extreme case, from the "waist" of a

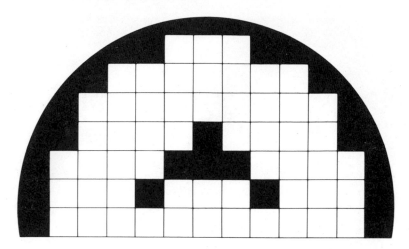

Figure 11-1 An arc "drawn" by the composer of a diagramless puzzle.

conventionally symmetric puzzle, the satisfaction in success is still greater. If an answer entered vertically proves incorrect, great is the joy in correcting the error. Temporary frustration is the basis of ultimate pleasure.

A diagramless puzzle may have conventional or some other form of symmetry—left-right like an "M" or top-bottom like a "B." You can combine this with or discard it for a pictographic representation of a thematic object. Diagrams shaped like a valentine and a six-pointed star were symmetric, while a map of New York State had no symmetry. Sharp points cannot be used, due to the limitation on how short an answer may be. You can simulate an arc of a circle however, by steps, as shown in Figure 11-1. Avoid long straight lines unless you have suitable long words in mind. You can break long lines with "fingers," strings of black squares, in some cases, without losing the pictographic effect. Thus a puzzle in the shape of the letter "W" is easy to construct, but the letter "T" is best forgotten. (See Figure 11-2 for an illustrative "K.")

Any theme suitable for use in a conventional puzzle can be used in a diagramless puzzle as well, but a diagramless puzzle is most appealing if its diagram carries out its theme. An outline can be a map (a state's border), a symbol ($, ℞, ♡ , or ✡), characters (such as 76 for the Bicentennial, or SA for South America), or a picture (a bunny's head, a telephone, or the Taj Mahal). Each outline readily suggests a related theme.

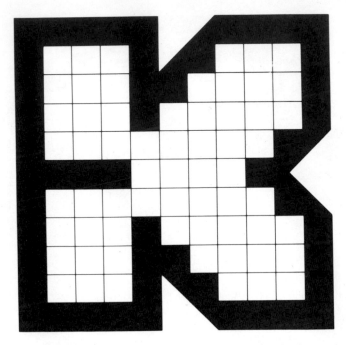

Figure 11-2   A diagramless puzzle in the shape of the letter "K" showing how you can "draw" diagonal lines and long straight lines.

Because connecting separate columns is a rewarding feat for solvers of diagramless puzzles, many such puzzles have outlines or portions that resemble the letter "W." This shape is a collection of "ladders," easy constructions for the composer. A diamond is another convenient shape, for the same reason. The composition of a pictographic puzzle with a long first word across is always a remarkable accomplishment.

Remember that the absence of a diagram may be but a slight impediment (spice) to seasoned solvers, but even they are due compensation. Obscurity must be avoided, definitions must be straightforward and reasonably unambiguous to hold the solver's attention and to be fair.

Gimmicks in the form of a few punny answers are acceptable, and certainly, themes unrelated to a diagram's shape are most common. Extreme deviousness, such as the use of symbols in answers, is unfair.

12
Composing Acrostic Puzzles

Put them all together, they spell MOTHER —H. Johnson,
"M-O-T-H-E-R, a Word that Means the World to Me"

Just as with crossword puzzles, construction of an acrostic puzzle proceeds from solution to definitions. In this chapter we discuss the selection of appropriate source quotations, the technique of puzzle construction, and the development of definitions.

CHOOSING A QUOTATION

Basics

There are three elementary rules:

1. The selection should evoke some reaction from the solver.
2. The selection *must* express a complete thought.
3. The quotation must contain all the letters used in the acrostic.

Nature of Material

The quotation may be purely objective or descriptive, like this excerpt from Ambrose Bierce's "A Horseman in the Sky":

> On a colossal pedestal, the cliff,—motionless at the extreme edge of the capping rock and sharply outlined against the sky,—was an equestrian statue of impressive dignity.

---

[1]It is sometimes possible for the composer to inject an *unobtrusive* word to supply a needed letter, but you should avoid this particular act of creativity if you can.

A humorous passage, especially one that combines humor with philosophy or description will usually be a good choice. This is from Mark Twain's "The Celebrated Jumping Frog of Calaveras County":

The new frog hopped off, but Dan'l gave a heave, and hysted up his shoulders—so—like a Frenchman, but it wasn't no use—he couldn't budge; he was planted as solid as an anvil, and he couldn't no more stir than if he was anchored out.

A quotation may also express some nugget of philosophy, as in these words by David Hume, from "Dialogues Concerning Natural Religion":

We know so little beyond common life, or even of common life, that, with regard to the economy of a universe, there is no conjecture, however wild, which may not be just; nor any one, however plausible, which may not be erroneous.

The possibilities are legion. Nontechnical descriptions of technical processes are suitable. Biographical and autobiographical anecdotes usually work well. Fiction and nonfiction, subjective passages, criticisms, prose and verse, all may serve.

Length

You must consider the quotation's length. An excerpt should be between 150 and 250 letters long, not counting punctuation. The first of the three selections above is not long enough.

The length of the acrostic is also important. It should be between 18 and 29 letters. If you have to, you can usually shorten the acrostic by using only the last name of the author, or by omitting an unimportant part of the title of the source material. Here are a few examples of shortened names and titles:

W. Shakespeare
Shakespeare
Adventures in Wonderland (The full title is *Alice's Adventures in Wonderland*)
"Philadelphia Story" (The full title begins with the word "The.")

The full acrostic for the second quotation would be far too long. We could shorten the title to "The Jumping Frog," which would result in a 23-letter acrostic. There is, however, an insurmountable problem with the selection. It contains no letter J—and that letter is needed even for the shortened acrostic.

The full acrostic for the quotation from Hume is 43 letters long. We use this quotation as a basis for technical discussion through the rest of the chapter, however, and so we shorten the acrostic by omitting the first two words in the title, so that the acrostic will spell: David Hume, "Natural Religion."

You should take into account the ratio between the total length of quotation and the length of the acrostic. Divide the number of letters in the quotation by the number of letters in the acrostic to find the length of the average word in the acrostic. If the result is less than six, the puzzle will probably be too easy to solve. If the result is greater than eight, you may have difficulty finding words you need. The Hume quotation has 179 letters. With a 24-letter acrostic the average word will be about 7½ letters long, just about ideal.

Sources of Material

Quotations can come from many sources. Most come from books, of course, but articles in magazines and journals are acceptable sources, as are titled speeches. Almost any published reading matter can supply appropriate quotations.

You must not overlook another source—your own imagination. Original material is accepted by most editors. Pointed, humorous verse is probably the most popular form of original writing for acrostic puzzles. Short filler paragraphs of the type used to pad newspaper columns usually aren't interesting enough to the solver. (If you do use original writing in an acrostic puzzle, the acrostic will spell your name. You will also have to supply a title for inclusion in the acrostic.)

We need to make some technical points here regarding sources.

1. The copyright laws generally permit the inclusion of brief excerpts in book reviews, and they also describe "fair use" so as to allow use of short selections for other purposes. They say nothing, however, about this specific use of copyrighted, material, except that you

should obtain written permission. You can avoid this minor incon-
venience, both for yourself and for the publishers, by sticking to
material for which copyright has expired, or which is in the public
domain. Don't worry, this limitation is not severe.

2. Be cautious about using "condensed" material. Go to an unabridged version and satisfy yourself that you have chosen the full
   version of a passage.
3. Don't use well-known excerpts. Solving should be a challenge up to
   some climactic moment. There's not much challenge in solving
   lines like "To be or not to be."
4. Newspaper articles, editorials, and wire-service writeups do not
   normally qualify as sources for acrostic puzzles because you cannot
   identify the author.
5. If you're going to use original writing, make sure it is just that—
   your own work. Don't get accused of plagiarism.

PUZZLE CONSTRUCTION

Foundation

The first step in construction of an acrostic puzzle, after the quotation is
selected, is to copy the passage onto a blank piece of paper, in large print.
While you're at it, write down the author's full name, the complete title of
the quotation's source, the publisher's name, the city of publication, and
the number of the page on which the quotation is found. (The last three
items are necessary when you submit the puzzle for sale.)

Next, count the letters in the quotation and jot down the total. Now
make a tally for *each* letter. As a double-check, add up these tallies and
compare the total to the one you've already written. If they don't match,
find and correct the error.

Now scan the individual tallies to see if there is a high incidence of any
of the less frequently encountered letters. If so, it's important that you
recognize the situation early; otherwise, you will have a lot of backtracking to do later. You should also look at the ratio of vowels to consonants to
know whether the words you use in the acrostic must have a prepon-
derance of either one.

The Hume quotation has 179 letters. The most frequent are: E-26,
O-23, and N-15. There are ten H's, eight W's, four V's, and two J's.
There are 103 consonants and 76 vowels, counting Y as a vowel. Although

O is a common letter, the tally is high and we will have to incorporate many O's early. The ratio of vowels to consonants is about three to four— not so uneven that we need to worry about it.

Framework

The next step is to write in a vertical line on another sheet of paper the letters that will start the acrostic. Adjust the letter tallies to account for these removed letters. (The only G in the Hume quotation is used in this step.)

Building

The most difficult step in composing an acrostic puzzle is the formation of words for the acrostic list using the letters in the quotation. Here are our rules:

1. You do not have to work sequentially through the acrostic. Skip around if that seems easier.
2. Morbid medical terms, and all the other words to be avoided in crossword puzzles, are out!
3. Keep in mind how long the average word must be, and make the first several words you form two or three letters longer than average. (Remember that the average word in the acrostic for our Hume quotation must be about 7½ letters long.)
4. In the initial stages hold back on vowels, S's, and D's, unless you are blessed with an abundance of these letters. You can always use S to make a noun plural or to change a verb to third person singular; D puts a verb into the past tense.
5. Use the "unusual" letters early, particularly any that occur often in your quotation. Some letters, especially H and W, occur more often in running prose than they do in a list of randomly chosen words. Prose ordinarily contains a few words like "the," "where," and "who" in comparative profusion, which accounts for this phenomenon.[2]

---

[2]Usually about half the letters that begin the acrostic will be vowels or the letters H or N. Since far fewer than half the words in the English language begin with these letters, those that do and that contain goodly numbers of "unusual" letters (including H and W) are very useful. Some of these are: HIGHHANDED, ANYHOW, INCHWORM, NOHOW, EREWHON (Samuel Butler's novel), EVERYWHERE, HOWEVER, HOTHOUSE, and UNWHOLESOME.

6. The mass market for acrostic puzzles, like that for crossword puzzles, favors single-word answers. Thus, you should avoid phrases and nonstandard words as much as possible. And, in this type of puzzle, with all the freedom you have as composer, you can do without variant spellings.[3]

Keeping Score

As you form a word for the acrostic, adjust the letter tallies to keep track of how many of each letter remains to be used. When you have made about half the number of words in the acrostic, recompute the length of the average word you will need to form from the remaining letters. Compute again when you're about three-quarters done. You should notice the average dropping. Of course, at the end you had better come out even.

Alternative Score-keeping Method

You may prefer this method of keeping track of the letters. Use tiles from a word game or make your own as we describe here:

Copy the quotation onto paper that you have ruled off into one-inch squares. After proofreading carefully to insure that you have copied the passage correctly, cut along the ruled lines to separate the individual letters. Now sort the squares into groups by letter and count each group to see if you need to "use up" any abundant unusual letters. To make words for the acrostic, start by laying out the letters that will be the initial letters of the word list. All you need do to form words is slide the remaining pieces of paper around until you make a satisfactory list. (If you're a "saver," you can keep the letters for use on your next puzzle.)

Thought Process

Figure 12-1 presents the Hume quotation, the letter tallies, and the acrostic we made from those letters. Here is the reasoning that led to formation of the first few words we made:

---

[3]The first acrostic puzzles were presented as literary challenges. The words in the acrostic were often phrases, lines from poems, from the Bible, and the like, with apt definitions. This aspect of acrostic puzzledom has by and large disappeared, with the exception of those puzzles written or edited by Thomas H. Middleton for his Simon and Schuster collections.

1. There are 23 O's and eight W's. (Ow!) 'HOW NOW BROWN COW' would get rid of four of each. Okay. ROOSEVELT uses up two more O's. NOW OR NEVER and THROW AWAY get rid of more of each.

2. There are two J's to dispose of. That's a lot in a quotation of this length. Put down ENJOYMENT, which also uses one of the five Y's, and INJECTION.

3. Put down LITHOSPHERE to use up two H's and another O. Try EFFECTIVE to work on the four F's and to use one of the four V's.

The last several words we made were UNITY, REEKS, INMATE, and LONER.

We know so little beyond common life, or even of common life, that, with regard to the economy of a universe, there is no conjecture, however wild, which may not be just; nor any one, however plausible, which may not be erroneous.

A	-7	D	emolish
B	-4	A	cheron
C	-7	V	owel
D	-3	I	mmune
E	-26	D	ebauchery
F	-4		
G	-1	H	ow now, brown cow
H	-10	U	tter
I	-10	M	ooch
J	-2	E	njoyment
K	-1		
L	-7	N	oodle
M	-7	A	bbot
N	-15	T	hrow away
O	-23	U	nity
P	-1	R	oosevelt
Q	-0	A	mnesty
R	-11	L	ithosphere
S	-6		
T	-12	R	eeks
U	-5	E	ffective
V	-4	L	oner
W	-8	I	njection
X	-0	G	houlish
Y	-5	I	nmate
Z	-0	O	ffice
	179	N	ow or never

Figure 12-1 Construction of an acrostic puzzle.

Finishing the Acrostic List

If you follow our building guidelines, especially #3, 4, and 5, the last
few words you need to form will perhaps be only three or four letters
long. They should contain a high percentage of easy-to-use letters. Thus,
your task should get easier near the finish. If you should get stuck, look
back at some of the *earliest* words you made, and regroup. Be extremely
careful at this stage if you are using pencil and paper to keep track of letter
tallies. It is incredibly easy to make a mistake and wind up with an extra
letter, or one too few. In fact, if you use pencil and paper to keep track,
you should double-check your work when you have made the complete
acrostic. Do this by reading through the acrostic list and tallying
individual letters, just as you first counted the letters in the quotation.
Compare the two sets of tallies. They must agree.

Completing the Composition

The next-to-last step in composing an acrostic puzzle is the association of
letters in the acrostic to letters in the quotation. The basic rule is that no
two letters from one word in the acrostic should appear in the same word
in the quotation. (Of course, if there is only one each of the letters Q and
U, you will have to violate this rule unless you managed to separate those
letters in the acrostic—for example, by using an Arabic word or place
name.)

Another rule, almost as important as the first, is that you should avoid
"clumping." It's a bad idea to wind up with letters from the first quarter
of the acrostic clumped in, say, the last quarter of the quotation. It makes
the puzzle too easy to solve, and it is tantamount to creating several
subpuzzles—just like a crossword puzzle diagram that does not interlock
completely.

Pursue this step methodically. You will be working with two things at
the same time: the quotation as you first copied it, and the acrostic you
formed from the letters in the quotation. Begin by numbering the letters in
the quotation. The first is *1*, next is *2*, and so on, in order through the
complete passage. Write these numbers under the letters in small print.

Next, identify each word in the acrostic by a letter, starting with A.
Write these letters to the left of the acrostic words.

Now, if your selection has a single occurrence of some letter (which

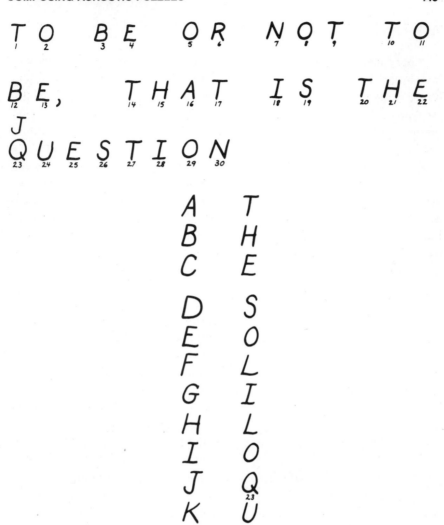

$$T \underset{1}{O} \quad B \underset{2}{E} \quad O \underset{5}{R} \quad N \underset{7}{O}T \quad T \underset{10}{O}$$

Figure 12-2   Assigning letters.

you can easily determine by checking your letter tallies), find that letter in the acrostic and in the quotation. Copy the identifier at the left of the acrostic word above the letter in the quotation. Copy the number that is underneath the letter in the quotation under the corresponding letter in the acrostic. Your work sheet should look like the example in Figure 12-2.

Notice the Q in "question" and in the acrostic word with identifier J. Deal at once with any other singly occurring letters.

Now find the longest word in the acrostic. Work carefully through that word to assign letters. A reasonable process is to find the first occurrence in the quotation of the first letter in the acrostic word, and assign that one by copying the identifier and number to their respective places. Then jump to the next word in the quotation and begin searching for the second letter in the acrostic word. When you have assigned all the letters in the acrostic word, keep your place in the quotation for searching, and locate the next acrostic word you want to deal with.

In general, you should assign the letters from the long acrostic words first. Conversely, you should go out of your way to leave one unassigned letter in every word of the quotation as long as possible. If you do so, you will have greater freedom towards the end; that is, you will almost always be able to find a letter you need without violating the basic rule about two letters in one acrostic word assigned to the same word in the quotation.

It is possible that you might hit a conflict when you get down to the last few words. If so, merely backtrack a few assignments. Be sure to correct your work sheets so that they reflect the final assignments.

Definitions

Preparing definitions for acrostic puzzles is just like preparing them for crossword puzzles, except that you can be a little wordier. This may open up some possibilities so that you can be a little less direct without being unfair.

Consider the word MINOR, for instance. An easy, direct clue would be "Under legal age." You are at liberty to incorporate two or more meanings for the same word in one definition. "Less important; type of chord" is fair and leads to MINOR, yet it is only one semicolon away from being a full-fledged cryptic clue.[4]

When you use a phrase or compound word in the acrostic list, tell the solver so by indicating "2 words" or "compound" after the definition. Publishers always give the solver this much help, even in difficult puzzles.

---

[4]Middleton occasionally includes acrostic puzzles with cryptic clues in his collections. Refer to Chapter 9 to learn how to write cryptic clues.

HOW LONG

It is easier to compose an acrostic puzzle than a crossword puzzle. We composed the model in this chapter in about 40 minutes. It incorporates three phrases, and perhaps it has a shortcoming in that nine words have double letters—although most editors wouldn't notice.

With practice, you can compose a good acrostic puzzle in one hour or less.

13
Marketing

Words pay no debts.—Shakespeare, *Troilus and Cressida*

In this chapter we discuss the mechanics of getting completed puzzles to market. The steps outlined here will probably seem tedious compared to the stimulation of composing puzzles. Yet, attention to detail is an important part of marketing puzzles, because *it's a buyer's market.*

That's it, in a nutshell. Puzzle publishers, whether they produce newsstand magazines, books, or newspaper features, receive more puzzles for consideration than they can use. You can take two steps to insure that your puzzles receive due consideration:

1. Send your work to suitable outlets. If you enjoy composing puzzles that have no themes, don't send them to a publication in which every puzzle is thematic. If you tend to write difficult puzzles or definitions, the newsstand magazines are not likely to accept your work.

   In short, read puzzle publications to see what they want.

2. Submit puzzles in accordance with guidelines or *style sheets* supplied by puzzle editors. These guidelines, which vary from editor to editor, standardize the format composers use to submit puzzles. Thus, the editor can concentrate on the puzzle's content without being distracted by typographical items. Editors are human, too, and want to make their jobs as simple as possible.

   You can obtain style sheets from most puzzle editors on request. Be sure to supply a stamped return envelope. (If you want to submit a puzzle to an editor who has not sent you a style sheet, use a puzzle from that editor's publication as a model for your submittal format.)

GENERAL GUIDELINES FOR SUBMITTING CROSSWORD PUZZLES

Squares in the puzzle diagrams you submit should be larger than publication size, say about one-third inch on a side. This reduces your writer's cramp and the editor's eyestrain. With squares this size, a 23 x 23 grid just fits on 8½" x 11" paper. You can prepare master grids using ordinary school notebook paper, which usually has three lines per inch. Trace grids of different sizes (15 x 15, 21 x 21, and 23 x 23, for instance) heavily onto sheets of plain white paper. Center each grid for a pleasing look on the page. Type your name, address, and Social Security Number in the upper right corner of each page. Make several copies of each grid at a copying service, and keep them on file.

Thoroughly darken the black squares in your pattern. Use pen and ink, soft-tipped pen, or a felt-tipped marker. (If you use a marker, which takes some practice, make sure the ink does not bleed through the page to discolor the underlying pages.) Check your work at this stage to make sure that you have darkened the correct squares.

Number the appropriate squares. Some editors demand that you use a typewriter. To paraphrase Tennyson: yours not to reason why, yours but to pacify. If you number by hand, use pen, not pencil.

Write the word count of your puzzle on the page. Here's a shortcut you can use to check the count, now that the pattern contains numbers. Count the number of squares that begin both Across and Down words. (These squares have a black square or a border above them and to the left of them.) Add this number to the number of the last word in the bottom row. The sum is your word count.[1]

Some editors (at the *New York Times*, for instance) want a diagram for their own use, for "trial solving." If the editor to whom you want to submit the puzzle wants a solving diagram, either get a copy of your diagram (at this stage) at a copying service or, if that's inconvenient, prepare a second diagram from scratch.

Complete the composition by filling in the answers, in capital letters. Again, some editors want you to use a typewriter. If you're working by hand, print legibly and use *pencil* unless the editor's guidelines instruct you otherwise. The editor has the right to change any part of the composition.

---

[1]Do you see why this is so? Every number is used for at least one answer. You have simply added to the number of the last word the number of times two answers have the same number.

8. Page size.   octavo
9. Low-starch bread   gluten (Am. Herit.)
10. Nebraska city   Omaha

Figure 13-1   Format for definitions and answers, including annotation.

Type definitions and answers as shown in Figure 13-1. Double space, and leave ample margins at the top, sides, and bottom of the page. Use one side of the page only. Some publications use periods after the numbers of the definitions, other do not. The editor will let you know if you use an unacceptable format. Type your name in the upper right corner of each page. You don't have to start a new page for the definitions for the Down words.

Identify the source of any obscure or unusual words. Do this briefly in parentheses after the word in the answer column, as illustrated in Figure 13-1. Some editors want this notation typed and others want it in pencil. (If you're not sure whether to annotate or not, do it.)

The editor's guidelines should indicate how to present certain kinds of definitions. For example, you indicate missing words in fill-in-the-blank definitions either by hyphens or underscores. Some publications help the solver by indicating "2 words" or "phrase" after the definition for a multiword answer, others do not.

Most crossword puzzles larger than 15 x 15 carry titles. Some publications even confer titles on 15 x 15 puzzles. Suggest a title for every puzzle you submit, especially if the puzzle is thematic. Of course, the editor is free to supply a substitute title.

Editors refer to crossword puzzles in correspondence (and on check stubs) either by title or by the answer at 1 Across.

GENERAL GUIDELINES FOR SUBMITTING ACROSTIC PUZZLES

The guidelines in the previous section apply to acrostic puzzles with some differences.

Individual squares in an acrostic puzzle's diagram should be larger than those in a crossword diagram, to hold the identifier as well as the numerals. Squares about one centimeter on a side are a good size. You can buy graph paper with one-centimeter rules.

A stockpile of master grids may not be of much use. Publishers print acrostic puzzles in different formats—15 squares per row, 17, 18, and so on. So be it. Match your submittal to the format your target publication commonly uses.

When you prepare the diagram, you should darken one square to represent the space between two words. It is probable that the quotation and dark squares will not exactly fill up the last row of the diagram. Simply darken the leftover squares in that row.

Identify your definitions by letters, not by numerals. The first identifier is "A," and they progress in alphabetic order. If your puzzle has more than 26 definitions, identify the 27th by "AA" or "Z1," depending on the style the editor prefers, the 28th by "BB" or "Z2," and so on.

Represent each letter in a word in the acrostic by three underscores, and type the proper numerals below, just as they appear in a magazine. (See Figure 13-2.) When a long word requires a second line of type, align the *right* margin, not the left. This keeps the sense of the acrostic clear. (Do the opposite for a telestich puzzle, one that uses the last letters of words instead of the first.)

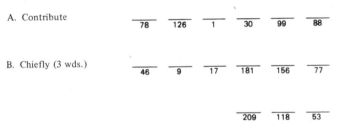

Figure 13-2   Format for acrostic puzzle definitions.

Submit four items as a complete solution to an acrostic puzzle:

1. Author's name and title of source material, in this form:

   Author: William Shakespeare
   Work: "Troilus and Cressida"

   Supply the author's full name and the complete title, even if you have omitted something to reduce the length of the acrostic.

2. Publisher's name and city, publication date, and page number of the quotation:

   Doubleday & Co., Inc., NY, 1936, page 838

3. The quotation itself: If you deliberately skipped an unimportant phrase to reduce the quotation's length, represent the missing part by an ellipsis (three periods).

4. Your acrostic composition: Type the word list, with identifiers, in two columns:

A. Demolish	L. Throw away
B. Acheron	M. Unity
. . .	. . .

All four parts of the solution will fit on a single page, along with your name, address, and Social Security Number.

ENCLOSURES

Enclose a self-addressed envelope, with enough postage to cover return of your puzzle. If you do not, you can never learn that your effort was unacceptable to one editor, and never be in a position to submit to another.

You can also write a short cover letter describing anything important you want to tell the editor about the puzzle—the nature of a concealed theme, perhaps. But don't be chatty just for the sake of being chatty.

REWARDS

When you asked someone what your blind date would be like and you heard something like, "great personality," you knew not to expect good looks. Well, so far as financial compensation is concerned, composing puzzles is really very, very enjoyable and educational, too.

Actually, you will derive two kinds of satisfaction from composing and selling puzzles. The first is intangible: seeing your name in print (if credit is given) and knowing that you are providing pleasure to a large number of people. The second satisfaction is monetary. The payment for a puzzle depends on two things—the size of the puzzle (for a crossword) and the nature of the publication.

In general, publishers of newsstand puzzle magazines and paperback books pay the least ($5 and up). Publishers of newspapers, including syndicators, and collections (such as the long-running Simon and Schuster series) pay more. *Games* Magazine, a "slick" publication devoted entirely to puzzles and games of all sorts, is probably the best-paying market today (up to $150).

Payment usually follows publication by about a week, but it can be a week or two early, as the *New York Times* often is, or several weeks later.

Some publishers (Simon and Schuster, for one) provide a nice fringe benefit: a complimentary copy of any collection in which your puzzle appears.

When you sell a puzzle, by the way, you warrant that it is original and that it has not been published before. You sell copyright, and all other rights including reprint rights. But you should receive a small additional payment if the publisher reprints the puzzle in a later collection.

Practically speaking, you have to treat puzzle composing as a hobby that pays for itself with something left over. Some editors make a good living. Some composers, with a great deal of persistence, have their works published regularly, and so they make a fair amount of money. As a casual constructor you cannot get rich ... but you can have a lot of fun trying.

MARKETS

There are three types of puzzle markets. The first is the small but growing "custom" market, in which puzzles are composed only when commissioned for specific audiences—for example, as personal gifts. At least two entrepreneurs are active in this market composing crossword puzzles; another composes original acrostic puzzles. Entry into this market requires the ability to reach potential customers through advertising, the talent for composing witty, heavily thematic puzzles using biographic or anecdotal information, and the know-how to present the finished product in a way that will itself be an advertisement. You cannot be successful in this market unless you have good business sense and can afford to work full time at it.

The second market includes special-interest publications such as magazines for hobbyists, magazines promoting geographical regions, and club newsletters. Some of these publications carry puzzles, either regularly or occasionally. A common characteristic of these publications is that they do not ordinarily have a "puzzle editor" per se. If you contribute to one of these publications, you must do a thorough job of proofreading your work—particularly the definitions. Investigate publications that do not now have a puzzle feature. If you have confidence in your ability to create enjoyable puzzles and meet regular deadlines, and you are willing to negotiate payment, you can become a regular contributor or "contributing editor" for an exclusive market.

A good way to keep abreast of special-interest publications that accept puzzles is to subscribe to "CWP," a newsletter for crossword puzzle constructors. CWP is published by W. J. Harrison Enterprises, P.O. Box 4282, San Rafael, CA 94903.

The third market includes general-interest publications that have a regular puzzle feature (newspapers and the syndicates that supply them), newsstand puzzle magazines, and collections of puzzles that book publishers produce. It is easier to break into this market than the first two, and, if you wish to compose puzzles only casually you will not be under the pressure of a deadline. Publications in this market are prepared to receive puzzles by new composers, and the editors will comment on puzzles and suggest improvements if they have time.

PUZZLE MARKET LIST

The alphabetic list of publishers and syndicators that follows covers only the third market mentioned above, and is not complete. New markets appear and established ones disappear. (The *New York Review of Books* began carrying an acrostic puzzle in September 1979. The *National Observer* ceased publication in 1977, after 15 years.) The omission of an active outlet from our list does not imply disapproval on our part. It means only that we are not aware of the outlet or that we do not have complete mailing information.

In most entries in the list, we supply the name of the current puzzle editor. Of course, editors are replaced from time to time. If you don't know the name of a publication's editor, send your contribution to the attention of the "Puzzle Editor." Some editors work for more than one publisher (for instance, a newspaper and a book series). They may instruct you to send contributions to their home addresses instead of the business addresses in our list.

We do not indicate actual payments. Amounts vary, and they are increasing. We encourage you to submit puzzles to many editors, to discover which editors like your work, and to decide which publications you want to contribute to on a regular basis.

And we wish you good luck!

Crosswords Editor,
Armor Publishing Co.,
120 East 56th Street,
New York, NY 10022.

Mr. Jack Looney,
Bantam Books,
666 5th Avenue,
New York, NY 10019.

Ms. Susan Hayes,
CBS Publications,
1515 Broadway,
New York, NY 10036.

Mr. Herb Ettenson,   (15 x 15, 23 x 23 and diagramless
c/o CTNYNS Syndicate,   puzzles)
220 East 42nd Street,
New York, NY 10017.

Mrs. Kathleen Rafferty,
Dell Publishing Co., Inc.
1 Dag Hammarskjold Plaza
New York, NY 10017.

Mr. Charles Preston,   (up to 23 x 23, and acrostic puzzles)
Doubleday Publishing Co.
245 Park Avenue,
New York, NY 10017.

Mr. Will Shortz,   (15 x 15 and larger)
GAMES Magazine,
515 Madison Avenue,
New York, NY 10022.

Mr. James Boldt,   (21 x 21)
(General Features Syndicate)
248 Canterbury Place,
Ridgewood, NJ 07450.

Ms. Joanne Goldstein,
JO-GO Publications,
P.O. Box 1086,
Reseda, CA 91335.

Mr. A. L. Herbert,
Official Publications,
641 Lexington Avenue,
New York, NY 10022.

Original Crosswords,
575 Madison Avenue,
New York, NY 10022.

Ms. Louise Barth,
Penny Press, Inc.,
P.O. Box 3211,
Stamford, CT 06905.

Mr. J. Quinn,
Quinn Publishing Co., Inc.,
855 S. Federal Highway,
Boca Raton, FL 33432.

Mrs. Margaret Farrar,   (up to 23 x 23, no acrostic puzzles)
c/o Simon & Schuster,
1230 Avenue of the Americas,
New York, NY 10020.

Mr. Thomas H. Middleton,   (acrostic puzzles only)
c/o Simon & Schuster,
1230 Avenue of the Americas,
New York, NY 10020.

Dr. Eugene T. Maleska,   (15 x 15, 21 x 21, 23 x 23, also
c/o The New York Times,   quotation puzzles 15 x 15 up to 23 x
229 West 43rd Street,   23, cryptic and diagramless puzzles)
New York, NY 10036.

Mr. Will Weng,   (17 x 17 up to 23 x 23)
c/o Times Books,
Three Park Avenue,
New York, NY 10016.

Appendix
Non-English Puzzles

You may use any language as you choose to indulge in without impropriety.—W. S. Gilbert, "Iolanthe"

Crossword puzzles are hardly a monopoly of English-speaking peoples. The sections below describe the characteristics of crossword puzzles as they appear in some European countries. They are identified by language because, for example, puzzles in the German language vary little in style among the German-speaking countries (although Switzerland is at least a near exception). All of the puzzles described below involve conventional definitions—as opposed to cryptic clues. This should not be surprising since the rampant borrowing that has shaped the English language has given it a richness, a wealth of synonyms, no other language approaches. It is precisely that wealth that facilitates the wordplay that is the essence of the clue.

Diagrams are quite another matter. Here, both conventional and cryptic patterns find few adherents. Perhaps because of patterns of inflection, puzzles in different languages have different types of diagrams.

FRENCH

The diagrams of French crossword puzzles (*mots croisés*, literally "crossed words") seem rather primitive and undisciplined compared to our own. (See Figure A-1.) They are only somewhat symmetric and need not be square. Unchecked letters are used, but usually no more than one in any one word. Words with as few as two letters are used. In fact, up to 20 per cent of a puzzle's entries may be that short. Puzzles are relatively small as a rule, say 9 x 9 or 9 x 11, with at least a few of the rows and columns containing only one word.

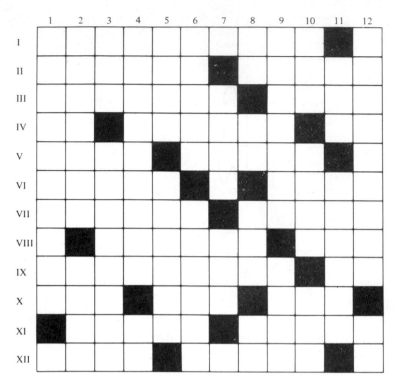

Figure A-1   A diagram for a French crossword puzzle.

Rows are most often designated by Roman numerals and columns by Arabic numerals. The definitions for a row or column are strung out, separated by periods or semicolons, after the designation of the row (*horizontalement*) or column (*verticalement*).

Definitions may be conventional or descriptive, that is, composed of a statement about the answer. Consecutive definitions may be related thematically or in form. There is usually no dominant theme for a puzzle. Descriptive and generic *(Abréviation)* definitions add difficulty. Abbreviations are used rather more frequently than in American puzzles.

Canadian puzzle fans enjoy bilingual crossword puzzles with English definitions for French answers and French definitions for English answers.

GERMAN

German crossword (*kreuzwort*) puzzles (*Rätsel*) are nonthematic. Each "black" square contains a definition of an indicated word that begins

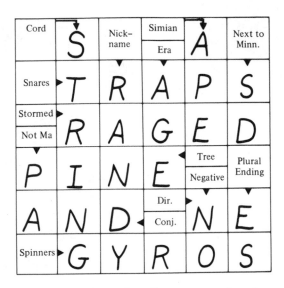

Figure A-2   A diagram for a German crossword puzzle.

nearby. (See Figure A-2.) One or two unchecked letters may appear in each word of the solution. The diagram has no symmetry. It is rectangular and often as large as about 10 x 24.

Variant German-language puzzles have diverse formats. A puzzle "*á la USA*" is square and symmetric like our modern crosswords, but has the unchecked letters we abandoned decades ago; definitions are listed as in French puzzles, albeit with only Arabic numerals; and no black squares, as in our diagramless puzzles. A *Kreuzwort á la France* is more faithful to the model, but larger. A *Schweden Kreuzwort* is also faithful to the original (see "Swedish" below) with cartoons in square cutouts within the basic rectangle—a Swedish diagram is otherwise hard to distinguish from a German one.

An appealing form uses the basic German diagram, but numbering like ours and unnumbered definitions, listed separately in random order for the words across (*waagrecht*) or down (*senkrecht*). The diagram is seeded with about 10 per cent of the solution's letters, none of them the most obvious. Some two-letter "words" may be undefined.

Like us, the Germans buy puzzle magazines that contain many types of puzzles, including fill-ins (puzzles with no definitions but with answers listed by length and alphabetically) and novel and more challenging forms. Definitions resemble ours in form. Two-letter words and abbreviations are fairly rare. An umlauted vowel (of which there are three in the

German alphabet) is entered as two letters, the second an "E." Puzzles occur widely in other publications, including pornographic magazines.

ITALIAN

Italian crosswords, *"parole incrociate"* (again, literally "crossed words") have rectangular diagrams that may have the symmetry like ours or none at all. (See Figure A-3.) Few words have more than one unchecked letter. Puzzles vary in size from about 10 x 11 to about 21 x 13. Numbers are placed as they are in our puzzles and the definitions, which are terse and similar to ours in every way, are listed like ours for words across (*orizzontali*) and down (*verticali*).

Novelty puzzles (all forms of which carry the word *cruciverba* in their names) include a diagramless variety, a bar crossword having thickened lines between squares to mark off words, puzzles with unnumbered and unordered definitions for all words, and pairs of puzzles that share the same rectangle and have an irregular border between them that the solver must discover. In this last form, definitions are listed in random order by puzzle and direction and a few letters and black squares are seeded. Puzzles with multiple letters per "square," like some published in England, are also found.

Long words are quite frequent in Italian puzzles and some beautiful fields of white, for example, 15 x 4, 10 x 5, and 9 x 8 (!), occur. Even distribution of vowels in Italian words and the absence of a requirement for symmetry seem to make these attractive patterns possible. Conversely, the fact that E appears often at the ends of English words and relatively rarely in other positions makes large fields of white rare in English-language crosswords.

SPANISH

Spanish crossword puzzles (*crucigramas*) come in many varieties. Diagrams are similar to those used in French, German, British (bar diagrams), or Italian crossword puzzles. Fields of white are smaller in Spanish crossword puzzles than in Italian puzzles: this is probably attributable to the fact that Spanish has fewer predominant word endings than Italian has. Definitions (*horizontales* and *verticales*) for most types of Spanish puzzles are identified and listed as they are in French puzzles.

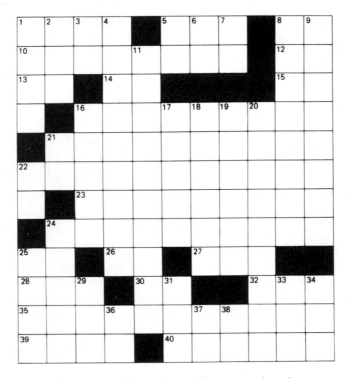

Figure A-3   A diagram for an Italian crossword puzzle.

Novelty puzzle forms include diagramless and acrostic puzzles like ours, and various syllable-oriented puzzles.

SWEDISH

As noted above, the diagrams of Swedish crossword (*Kryss*) puzzles resemble those of the standard German variety, with rectangular cutouts. What makes them most appealing, however, is that each cutout contains a photograph or cartoon for which a caption or punchline appears in the solution, either as a single entry or snaking along an indicated path among standard entries. Definitions in the squares that we would blacken make numbers unnecessary. Unchecked letters are used very sparingly, but two-letter words are relatively common. Long words are common, but fields of white are rare.

Definitions are conventional in the type of puzzle described above, but another type of puzzle is also common. The latter type has a smaller diagram like that of a standard cryptic puzzle and definitions that tend somewhat to the same obliqueness.

SUMMARY

Some European crosswords may seem inferior to ours in some ways, but poverty of vocabulary in languages more insular or more resistant to borrowing may well account for that. On the other side of the ledger, even American and British magazines seem not to have discovered foreign forms, varying only slightly from our own, that might yield solvers and composers great pleasure in decades to come. As in all things, people eventually learn that "different" hardly implies "inferior" and cultural crossbreeding most often works to everyone's advantage.

GLOSSARY

ACROSTIC—A verse or list of words in which the first letters taken in order spell something significant. In an *acrostic puzzle*, the acrostic spells the name of the author, and, usually, the name of a book from which a quotation incorporated in the puzzle was taken. See also *telestich*.

ACROSTIC PUZZLE—A puzzle form invented by Mrs. Elizabeth Kingsley, consisting of a quotation or excerpt from some published work, which the solver must discover with the help of definitions; the definitions lead to words made up from the letters in the quotation. The puzzle indicates where in the quotation the letters in the defined words are to be written. The defined words form an *acrostic*, or, rarely, a *telestich*.

ANAGRAM—A word formed from the reordered letters of another word or words.

ANSWER—That which is entered into a conventional crossword puzzle's *diagram* in satisfaction of a *definition*; analogous to *light*. Also, the solution of a *clue* in some varieties of cryptic puzzles; the solver must apply a *transformation* to change such an answer into a *light*.

BLACK SQUARE—A square in a puzzle, darkened or otherwise differentiated to indicate that no letter is to be entered into it. It marks the beginning or end of an *answer, light,* or word of a *quotation*. The border of a crossword puzzle functions similarly.

BLIND CORNER—A portion of a crossword puzzle's *diagram* connected to the remainder of the puzzle's diagram by no more than one *answer* or *light*.

BOX QUOTE—A crossword puzzle form devised by Eugene T. Maleska. In this form of puzzle, a quotation is to be discovered by the solver. The quotation is found running clockwise in rectangular fashion in the interior of the diagram. Like the *Step-Quote*, the Box-Quote typically contains the author's name and the title of the source of the quotation in the diagram.

CHARADE—A building up of a *light* by bits and pieces, that is, by sets of letters, a type of a *hint*.

CHEATER—A *black square* whose absence would not alter a puzzle's *word count*, and whose presence simplifies the composer's task.

CIRCLES-IN-THE-SQUARE—A crossword puzzle form devised by Eugene T. Maleska. In this form of puzzle, a quotation is to be discovered by the solver. The letters in the quotation are strewn, in order, through the diagram; the squares in the diagram that contain these letters are indicated by inscribed circles. Like the *Step-Quote*, a Circles-in-the-Square typically contains the author's name and the title of the source of the quotation.

CLUE—That which is provided to lead the solver to a *light* in cryptic and humorous puzzles; like *definition*, but connoting wordplay in addition to a conventional, although usually camouflaged, definition.

COCKNEY—A dialect of London in which initial H's are dropped and initial vowels are preceded by H's, used in *definitions by model*.

COMPOSER—The one who devises a puzzle; also "compiler" or "constructor." See also *editor*.

CORNER—A rectangular region of a diagram, typically one bounded by the puzzle's border on one side or two sides, and *fingers* on two additional sides.

COMPOSITION—A puzzle's diagram with its *answers* or *lights* inserted.

CRAZY CROSSWORD—A humorous puzzle composed by Ted Shane or his successors.

CRYPTIC PUZZLE—A crossword puzzle whose *lights* are found through *clues* rather than *definitions*.

DEFINITION—That which is provided to lead the solver to an *answer* in a conventional puzzle; like a *clue*; also the part of a clue that serves the same purpose.

DEFINITION BY CLASS—A *definition* in which a category is given, of which the *answer* is an example; "Vine" is a definition by class for IVY.

DEFINITION BY EXAMPLE—A *definition* in which examples of the class named by the answer are given; "Princetonian or Columbian" is a definition by example for IVY.

DEFINITION BY MODEL—A *definition* in which a manner of language is used that is to be aped in deriving the answer, for example, Cockney, a lisp, abbreviation; "Hitchy" is a far-fetched definition for IVY (meaning " 'aving 'ives").

DIAGRAM—A puzzle's squares in which letters are to be entered.

DIAGRAMLESS PUZZLE—A crossword puzzle with no *diagram* given, only a list of *definitions* (appropriately numbered) and the dimensions of its rectangular *grid*.

DIMENSION—The number of squares in one row or column of a puzzle's rectangular *grid*.

DOUBLE ENTENDRE—A crossword puzzle having two equally valid *solutions*.

EDITOR—One who receives puzzles from *composers* and prepares them for publication; therefore, one, unlike a *composer*, to whom puzzles can constitute more than merely a hobby.

FIELD OF WHITE—Rectangle comprising only white squares.

FILL-IN-THE-BLANK—A *definition* consisting of a phrase in which the *answer* has been omitted.

FINGER—Two or more black squares perpendicular to and abutting a border of a *grid*.

GRID—The rectangular arrangement of squares that contains a puzzle's *diagram*.

HINT—That portion of a *clue* that leads to the *light* by an indirect route involving some type of wordplay.

HOMOGRAPH—The use in a clue of a word that is spelled just like another, unrelated, more common word. Other words in the clue lead the solver to think first of the unrelated word, not the word that leads to the light. Examples of words used in this way are: sewer (one who sews), number (having less feeling), wicked (having a wick), and flower (that which flows, a river).

HUMOROUS PUZZLE—An American crossword puzzle, made up of ordinary words, with imaginative clues. The clues employ wit, anagrams, puns, and other types of wordplay, rather than standard "dictionary" definitions. See *Crazy Crossword, Puns and Anagrams,* and *Puns and Twists.*

LADDER—A diagonal arrangement of black squares within a *diagram*; also the (equal-length) *answers* between two such ladders.

LIGHT—That which is entered into a cryptic crossword puzzle's diagram in satisfaction of a *clue*; like the conventional *answer*.

LISP—The use of TH for a sibilant sound; used in *definitions by model*.

NOM DE PUZZLE—A *composer's* pseudonym.

NUMBER—The integer associated with a *definition, clue, answer,* or *light*.

PANGRAMMATIC—Having every letter of the alphabet (in the solution of a puzzle).

PATTERN—A *grid* with *black squares*. A pattern with numbers inserted is a *diagram*.

PICTOGRAPHIC—Having a *diagram* whose outline is suggestive of the puzzle's theme; said of a *diagramless puzzle*.

PUNS AND ANAGRAMS—A *humorous puzzle* published in *The New York Times*, 15 x 15 with a word count below 73.

PUNS AND TWISTS—A form of *hunorous puzzle* published in *The New York Times*, 17 x 13 with a word count below 73.

PUZZLE—A composition and its associated *definitions* or *clues*.

PUZZLE WORD—A word that is encountered by most solvers only in puzzles, for example, ERS (a bitter vetch).

QUOTATION—What is to be entered into the *diagram* of an *acrostic puzzle*.

REBUS—A thematic *answer* containing a symbol, that is, something other than an alphabetic character, that the solver must enter into a square.

RELOCATED THEME—A puzzle's theme carried out by the *definitions* of the longest *answers* rather than by the answers themselves.

SIGNAL—That part of a *clue's hint* that indicates the form of wordplay used in the hint.

SKELETON—That portion of a unfinished *composition* formed by chosen thematic *answers*.

SLIDE-QUOTE—A crossword puzzle form devised by Eugene T. Maleska. In this form of puzzle, a quotation is to be discovered by the solver. The quotation runs diagonally from the upper left-hand corner of the diagram to the lower right-hand corner. Like the *Step-Quote*, the Slide-Quote typically contains the author's name and the title of the source of the quotation in the solution.

SOLUTION—*Composition* as seen by a solver.

SPINE—A long *answer* in the middle of the central row or column of a *diagram*.

SQUARE DEALING—Following the precepts of Afrit, Ximines, and Azed regarding cryptic clues. Every square-dealing clue is grammatically precise and contains both a *definition* of the answer and a *hint*.

STEP-QUOTE—A crossword puzzle form devised by Eugene T. Maleska. In this form of puzzle, a quotation is to be discovered by the solver. The quotation begins at "1 Across" and makes its way through the diagram in a stair-step fashion ending in the lower right-hand corner. Typically, the puzzle also contains the author's name and title of the source of the quotation.

STYLE SHEET—A statement of an editor's requirements, including maximum word counts, formats to be used in submitting puzzles, etc.

TELESTICH—A verse or list of words in which the last letters, taken in order, spell something significant. See also *acrostic*.

TRANSFORMATION—In some varieties of cryptic puzzles, what the solver must apply to an *answer* to convert it to a *light*. In a "Letters Latent" cryptic, for example, the solver must omit one letter from each answer in the course of filling in the solution.

UNCH—An *unch*ecked letter, that is, one appearing in only one *light*.

WORD COUNT—The number of *answers* or *lights* in a crossword puzzle.